RED

RED

Passion and Patience in the Desert

Terry Tempest Williams

PANTHEON BOOKS • NEW YORK

Notices of previous publication and permissions acknowledgments
appear on pages 257–58.

Pantheon Books and colophon are registered trademarks of Random House, Inc.

Library of Congress Cataloging-in-Publication Data

Williams, Terry Tempest
Red: passion and patience in the desert / Terry Tempest Williams.
p. cm.
Contents: Home Work—Coyote's Canyon—Red—Desert quartet—Wild mercy.
ISBN 0-375-42077-0
1. Utah—Description and travel.   2. Natural history—Utah.
3. Human ecology—Utah.   4. Utah—Environmental conditions.
5. Deserts—Utah—Psychological aspects.   6. Wilderness areas—Utah—
Psychological aspects.   7. Williams, Terry Tempest—Philosophy.   I. Title.

F830.W55 2001   333.78′4—dc21   2001021456

www.pantheonbooks.com

Book design by Fearn Cutler

Endpaper map created by Chalk Butte Digital Maps.
Map on page 233 by Fred Swanson.

Printed in the United States of America

2 4 6 8 9 7 5 3

333.78
WIL

For

The Coyote Clan

and

America's Redrock Wilderness

Eyeglances, whose winks
no brightness sleeps.
Undebecome, everywhere,
gather yourself,
stand.

—Paul Celan,
Threadsuns

CONTENTS

Home Work   1

Coyote's Canyon   21

Red   59

Desert Quartet   193

Wild Mercy   213

Appendices   217

America's Redrock Wilderness Act   219
Map of America's Redrock Wilderness   233
America's Redrock Wilderness: The Citizens' Proposal   235
Supporting Organizations   245

Acknowledgments   251

HOME WORK

Home Work

It is a simple equation: place + people = politics. In the American West, the simplicity becomes complicated very quickly as abstractions of philosophy and rhetoric turn into ground scrimmages—whether it's over cows grazing on public lands, water rights, nuclear waste dumps in the desert, the creation of the Grand Staircase–Escalante National Monument, or the designation of wilderness. This territory is not neutral. The redrock desert and canyon country of southern Utah provokes powerful divisive opinions.

How are we to find our way toward conversation?

For me, the answer has always been through story. Story bypasses rhetoric and pierces the heart. Story offers a wash of images and emotion that returns us to our highest and deepest selves, where we remember what it means to be human, living in place with our neighbors.

I came to the stories in "Coyote's Canyon" through a question: "What stories do we tell that evoke a sense of place?" I had just finished a long inquiry into Navajo oral tradition and had been working on the reservation in various public schools. It was clear to me, both the elders and children alike had deep ties to the land through story. Whether it was Shiprock, Window Rock, or the ruins at Hovenweep, each landform, each significant site, seemed to have a name accompanied by a story. The stories they told animated the country, made the landscape palpable and the people accountable to the health of the land, its creatures, and each other. This is not to romanticize the Diné (as they call themselves), only to voice my profound respect for their intricate and complex cosmology.

How do the stories we tell about ourselves in relationship to place shape our perceptions of place? Is there room for a retelling of our own creation stories, even Genesis?

In the Colorado Plateau—roughly the Four Corners region of Utah, Colorado, New Mexico, and Arizona—I believe we are in the process of creating our own mythology, a mythology born out of this spare, raw, broken country, so frightfully true, complex, and elegant in its searing simplicity of form. You cannot help but be undone by its sensibility and light, nothing extra. Before the stillness of sandstone cliffs, you stand still, equally bare.

These redrock canyons in southern Utah are an acquired taste. They are short on water and, as a result, short on green. Green recalls pastoral comfort, provides a resting place for the eyes. There are moments when I long for the canopy and cover of a forest to hide in, to breathe in, to breathe with, and delight in the growing shades and patterns of green. I never forget I inhabit the desert, the harsh, brutal beauty of skin and bones.

Although we have mountains here of extraordinary stature and elevations—the LaSals in particular, rising to twelve thousand feet—the high points of excursions into the Colorado Plateau are usually points of descent. Down canyons. Down rivers. Down washes left dry, scoured, and sculpted by sporadic flash floods.

It's tough country to visit. It's even tougher country to live in. So powerful is the sun in summer, one adopts a perpetual squint. Summer can bring biblical periods of forty days of heat well over one hundred degrees, reducing you to a lizard state of mind, no thought and very little action. You sleep more and you dream. It is a landscape of extremes. You learn sooner or later to find an equilibrium within yourself; otherwise, you move.

Desert as teacher.

Desert as mirage.

Desert as illusion, largely our own.

What you come to see on the surface is not what you come to know. Emptiness in the desert is the fullness of

space, a fullness of space that eliminates time. The desert is
time, exposed time, geologic time. One needs time in the
desert to see.

As the world becomes more crowded and corroded by
consumption and capitalism, this landscape of minimalism
will take on greater significance, reminding us through its
blood red grandeur just how essential wild country is to
our psychology, how precious the desert is to the soul of
America.

These lands have been here for millions of years, and
they will certainly outlast us by another million years or
more. But they will not remain ecologically intact without
our vigilance, without our willingness to protect what is
wild.

Those of us who live here know the heartbreak of
loss. Since the construction of the Glen Canyon Dam,
which shunted the flow of the Colorado River on its way
toward the Grand Canyon in the 1950s, as residents of the
Desert West, we have learned wildness cannot be taken for
granted. It's not just the loss of a "playground" or a place of
recreation, as many opponents would argue; it's the funda-
mental loss of natural systems, free-flowing rivers, rock art
pecked and painted into stone by the hands of the Ancient
Ones a thousand years ago. It is the drowning of a way of

life, the death of natural communities that are much older, and perhaps wiser, than those of our own species.

Most lands in the American West are public lands, a commons if you will, held inside a national trust: national forests, Bureau of Land Management lands, national parks, monuments, and refuges. Only a small portion of our lands are privately owned, 22 percent in the state of Utah. Our character is shaped by the rugged truth of indifference— mountain ranges and arid basins, sagebrush oceans, grass- lands, high deserts and plateaus, wild and raging rivers. It's hard to take yourself very seriously when confronted face- to-face with a mountain lion or the reality of no water in the desert. There's so much land, stretches of land so vast you cannot see it all at once, certainly not in a lifetime. We stand under the canopy of stars and are flushed with humil- ity, stars no longer seen by most as they are erased by urban life.

The region of the American West shares common ground with the South: each has found its voice in loss. The South was forever shaped by the Civil War, and today we in the West are in the midst of our own. It is not a bat- tle over issues of slavery. It is a battle over public and pri- vate uses of land, what will be developed and what will remain sovereign. Guns are replaced by metaphorical mon- key wrenches and shovels.

In November 1999 the watchdog group Public Employees for Environmental Responsibility issued a report saying, "beatings, bombings, death threats, and other incidents against federal resource employees, largely in the West, have been steadily rising since 1995." *Audubon* reported in their January–February 2000 issue that "In 1998 there were almost 100 incidents in which the personnel or buildings of the U.S. Forest Service, Bureau of Land Management, and other agencies were targets of physical attack, destruction, or a direct threat of violence."

Hostilities became so great in Elko County, Nevada, that Gloria Flora resigned as supervisor of the Humboldt–Toiyabe National Forest in Nevada, the largest national forest in the lower forty-eight. She feared for the safety of her employees and wanted to shed light on the abuses. A rising star in the Forest Service, she left her post in protest in November 1999.

In an attempt to rescue the last viable population of bull trout from extinction, Flora moved to permanently close a dirt road that had been washed out in a flood. This created a firestorm among ranchers in the community, who vowed to bulldoze a new road—one that biologists said would be detrimental to the trout. Only after a federal judge intervened with a last-minute restraining order did the locals retreat from scraping out a new road.

But the next generation of Sagebrush Rebels have not given up. On July 4, 2000, hundreds of protestors from around the West gathered in Elko to form "the Jarbidge

Shovel Brigade," yet another action to defy the U.S. Forest Service. With shovels in hand, they were determined to open the Bull Trout road, now more symbolic than real. "We will rebuild the road, come hell or high water," declared Tony Lesperance, an Elko County commissioner. Following the action was a parade designed to fuel the passions of those who not only distrust the federal government but despise it for interfering in their backyard, complete with a float bearing a tombstone that read "U.S. Forest Service."

The second section of *Red* focuses on the idea of wildness and specifically the wilderness of southern Utah. I have added to this mix of essays, congressional testimony, newspaper clippings, and journal entries, to create both a chronology and collage for the reader, to feel the swell of a community trying to speak on behalf of wild places that are threatened by development or legislation in the United States Congress. In 1995 Representative James V. Hansen (R-Utah) and Senator Orrin Hatch (R-Utah) introduced the Utah Public Lands Management Act, which would have designated 1.7 million acres as wilderness out of 22 million acres of BLM lands. That bill was defeated in 1996 in the United States Senate.

Six months later President Clinton, on the rim of the Grand Canyon, created the Grand Staircase–Escalante National Monument through the authority of the 1906 Antiquities Act, setting aside for future posterity almost two million acres of wildlands. There are people in the state of Utah who are still infuriated by that gesture, protesting that folks in rural Utah had no voice in the process. And threats continue to be made by Republican leaders such as Dick Cheney to overturn the decision. It was no different sixty years ago, in Jackson Hole, Wyoming, when the Grand Teton National Monument was established. Federal control in the American West remains an open wound.

With the election of George W. Bush as president of the United States, Gale Norton as the secretary of interior (a protégé of former secretary of interior James Watt under the Reagan administration), and Representative Jim Hansen from Utah as the powerful chairman of the Natural Resources Committee, there will be no dearth of creative and cutthroat attempts to undermine and undo much of Clinton's environmental legacy, such as the Grand Staircase–Escalante National Monument in Utah and the National Forest Roadless Area Conservation Rule that protects nearly sixty million acres of national forest in thirty-eight states, including the Tongass in southeast Alaska.

In an eight-page letter sent to President-elect Bush on December 27, 2000, Congressman Hansen wrote: "After many years of being frustrated by the Clinton administration's unreasoned and frequently absurd interpretation of law and congressional intent, I am elated at finally having the opportunity to work with your administration to correct the misguided direction the Clinton administration has taken in their attempt to manage our natural resources."

According to the January 4, 2001, issue of the *Washington Post,* suggestions outlined in Hansen's letter included "everything from relaxing restrictions on snowmobile use in some national parks to removing some of the national monument designations the president had given public lands in recent years."

I believe Aldo Leopold was correct when he wrote in *A Sand County Almanac* in 1949:

No important change in ethics was ever accomplished without an internal change in our intellectual emphasis, loyalties, affections, and convictions. The proof that conservation has not yet touched these foundations of conduct lies in the fact that philosophy and religion have not yet heard of it. In our attempt to make conservation easy, we have made it trivial.

As an American writer, I have found no subject to be as intellectually challenging as writing about wilderness. How can I convey the scale and power of these big wide-open lands to those who have never seen them, let alone to those who have? How can I learn to write out of my own experience, out of my deep love for wild country, while still maintaining a language that opens minds rather than closes them? How to write again and again from every conceivable angle to stay the hand of development? How to write as clearly as one can from the heart and still be credible?

In the middle of the Utah wilderness campaign in 1996, Mary Page Stegner sent some inspiriting words by her late husband, Wallace Stegner, about why paving the Burr Trail outside Capitol Reef National Park was a wrong-headed idea:

Why? So people coming up dammed Glen Canyon in power boats can get out of the water and make it more easily from ramp to ramp. And anyone on the fringes of that lovely stone wilderness will hear their motors ten, fifteen, twenty miles away across the garbed stone, reverberating off the Kaiparowits Cliffs, ricocheting off the Waterpocket Fold.

As there has been nothing to interrupt the silence in this desert, so there is nothing to break the view of watercourses, of cliff lines and gulch and bare bald heads and domes, so there will be nothing to intercept the view of cut and fill highway.

This road as proposed by the Utah highway commission, would be a tragedy, the dimmest of "wilderness breaking." Poverty program, public works? Yes—poverty of intelligence, poverty of imagination, poverty of sensibility. And a greater poverty for Utah's future, once that last wilderness is split, shattered, and brought down to size.

—Wallace Stegner
Unpublished journal entry, 1966

The issue of Utah wilderness has not gone away; nor has it been resolved. There is now a bill before Congress known as America's Redrock Wilderness Act. In the spring of 1999, this new and improved bill was reintroduced in Congress designating 9.1 million acres, up from the previous 5.7 million acres in 1995, after Representative Hansen himself called for a reinventory of all BLM lands under consideration for wilderness. This was done under the supervision of the Department of Interior. As of this date, there is bipartisan support for America's Redrock Wilderness Act with 144 cosponsors in the House of Representatives and 12 cosponsors in the Senate.

Representative Maurice Hinchey (D-NY), who reintroduced the bill in the 107TH Congress on April 26, 2001, stated: "The redrock wilderness is already owned by all the people of the United States and should be considered a national treasure like the Grand Canyon or the Statue of Liberty.... This terrain cannot bear much use or development, and the treasures it holds are too rare and special to be exploited."

Ironically, as this speech was being uttered in the halls of Congress, the Bush administration was drafting plans to open 17 million acres of public lands in 11 western states, now designated as sensitive wilderness study areas (wsa's), with as much as 3 million acres in Utah alone, for the possibility of oil and gas development.

Other pieces of legislation in the form of smaller, regional wilderness bills are also under consideration. The San Rafael Swell Bill, sponsored by Representative Chris Cannon (R-Utah) and Jim Hansen, is an example of this land parceling strategy. This bill has lost squarely on the House floor but is sure to be resurrected under the new Bush administration. These bills, which set land aside piecemeal and with less protective measures, are not supported by conservation groups such as the Southern Utah Wilderness Alliance, the Utah Wilderness Coalition, The Wilderness Society, or the Sierra Club.

And so the civil war continues.

For all our efforts, collectively within the state of Utah and outside it, we still have no wilderness designation on BLM lands. While we wait, wild Utah is being whittled away like every other state in the West with increasing off-road vehicle use, threats of oil and gas drilling, and State Institutional Trust Lands being sold to the highest bidder, leading to the escalation of trophy homes, gated communities, and luxury resorts often near the boundaries of national parks and wilderness areas.

But this is not to say that finding common ground is impossible. Out of chaos, creativity is emerging. We in the American West are coming of age. Progress is being made within rural communities as watershed councils and local land trusts are being formed, enlisting creative partnerships in the name of land stewardship. In my own town of Castle Valley, Utah, residents have organized the Castle

Rock Collaboration, its primary purpose to protect over five thousand acres of open space owned by the State Institutional Trust Lands Administration, which has a mandate to develop it. These wildlands sit between three wilderness study areas: Fisher Towers, Mary Jane Canyon, and Porcupine Rim and Morning Glory Canyon. If this buffer zone is compromised, not only will wilderness be compromised but also the integrity of this village in the desert. The residents of Castle Valley have repeatedly said through a majority vote that they do not want any commercial development. It is a local community engaged in its own self-determination in choosing how to live in place, struggling to "create a society to match the scenery."

There are other sustainable development initiatives gaining favor, such as supporting ranchers by buying locally grown beef or purchasing value-added timber products from small-scale logging companies mindful of harmful forestry practices such as clear-cutting. Many ranchers who once overgrazed public lands are today practicing methods of holistic range management, just as family logging operations are now harvesting trees more selectively. These are just a few examples of a changing West. But it is slow and arduous and requires the patience of stone. Meanwhile, the great beast of progress continues to make its tracks upon the wilderness.

If a sense of place can give rise to a politics of place, where might an erotics of place lead?

In "Desert Quartet," I explore the landscape of love in elemental form: Earth, Fire, Water, Air. I wanted to create a narrative that experimented with the question of what it might mean to make love to the land, not in an exploitive manner or a manner of self-indulgence but in a manner that honors our relationship to Earth, deep, primal, enduring.

Our traditional use of the word *erotic* has been coupled with images of pornography and voyeurism. I am interested in a participatory relationship with the land. I want to reclaim the word *erotic* at its root, meaning "of or pertaining to the passion of love; concerned with or treating of love; amatory."

For those who have wandered through the serpentine canyons of the Escalante, floated down the Green and Colorado Rivers, biked the White Rim Trail in Canyonlands, or hidden out for days along the Dirty Devil or stood below Morning Glory Arch in winter or thought they found God in the expanse of the Kaiparowits Plateau, this is not hard to understand: falling in love with a place, being in love with a place, wanting to care for a place and see it remain intact as a wild piece of the planet.

Shortly before his death, T. H. Watkins, a distinguished writer and lover of southern Utah, wrote:

. . . maybe, just maybe, before the last little town is cor-
rupted and the last of the unroaded and undeveloped wildness
is given over to dreams of profit, maybe it will be love, finally,
love for the land for its own sake and for what it holds of
beauty and joy and spiritual redemption, that will make the
redrock country of southern Utah not a battlefield but a revela-
tion.

For those who have not experienced the sublime nature
of Utah's canyon country, I invite you to imagine what it
might be like to see and feel the world from the inside out.
If you do come visit, prepare to be broken open like a rock
fallen from a once-secure place.

For those who do know and love the Colorado Plateau,
may these stories be a reminder of pink sand underfoot
and ravens overhead and the joyous sensation of finding
red dirt in every pore of your skin. May you recall the
transformative power of wildness and remember it survives now only through vigilance.

I believe that spiritual resistance—the ability to stand
firm at the center of our convictions when everything
around us asks us to concede—that our capacity to face the
harsh measures of a life, comes from the deep quiet of listening to the land, the river, the rocks. There is a resonance
of humility that has evolved with the earth. It is best retrieved in solitude amidst the stillness of days in the desert.

A friend of mine said to me recently after visiting the slickrock country of southern Utah, "What a pity, wilderness has become irrelevant before it has become resolved."

Alan Freemyer, an aide to Resource Committee chair Representative Hansen, said after the reintroduction of America's Redrock Wilderness Act in 2001, "Frankly, the Red Sox have a better chance of winning this year's World Series than this bill has of becoming law."

And there are those who are saying, very thoughtfully, that it will only be by eliminating our desire to set land aside as "wilderness" that we can begin to regard all landscapes with respect and dignity.

I understand these points of discussion. In an ideal world, a world we might well inhabit one day, we may not need to "designate" wilderness, so evolved will be our collective land ethic, our compassion for all manner of life, so responsive and whole. We will not have to "preserve" or "protect" land because we will have learned what it means to be "good stewards," to see the larger community as an embrace of all species. I pray there will indeed come a time, when our lives regarding the domestic and the wild will be seamless.

But we are not there yet.

In the meantime, what are we to do?

I choose to err on the side of preservation, and stand shoulder to shoulder with brothers and sisters in our shared desire to protect the last, large expanses of wilderness we have left.

Once strengthened by our association with the wild, we can return to family and community. Each of us belongs to a particular landscape, one that informs who we are, a place that carries our history, our dreams, holds us to a moral line of behavior that transcends thought. And in each of these places, home work is required, a participation in public life to make certain all is not destroyed under the banner of progress, expediency, or ignorance. We cannot do it alone. This is the hope of a *bedrock democracy,* standing our ground in the places we love, together.

Red is a gesture and bow to my homeland.

I want to write my way from the margins to the center. I want to speak the language of the grasses, rooted yet soft and supple in the presence of wind before a storm. I want to write in the form of migrating geese like an arrow pointing south toward a direction of safety. I want to keep my words wild so that even if the land and everything we hold dear is destroyed by shortsightedness and greed, there is a record of beauty and passionate participation by those who saw what was coming.

Listen. Below us. Above us. Inside us. Come. This is all there is.

COYOTE'S CANYON

These things are real: desert, rocks, shelter, legend.

—Judith Fryer

The Coyote Clan

When traveling to southern Utah for the first time, it is fair to ask, if the redrocks were cut would they bleed. And when traveling to Utah's desert for the second or third time, it is fair to assume that they do, that the blood of the rocks gives life to the country. And then after having made enough pilgrimages to the slickrock to warrant sufficient separation for society's oughts and shoulds, look again for the novice you once were, who asked if sandstone bleeds.

Pull out your pocketknife, open the blade, and run it across your burnished arm. If you draw blood, you are human. If you draw wet sand that dries quickly, then you will know you have become part of the desert. Not until then can you claim ownership.

This is Coyote's country—a landscape of the imagination, where nothing is as it appears. The buttes, mesas, and redrock spires beckon you to see them as something other:

a cathedral, a tabletop, bear's ears, or nuns. Windows and arches ask you to recall what is no longer there, to taste the wind for the sandstone it carries. These astonishing formations invite a new mythology for desert goers, one that acknowledges the power of story and ritual yet lies within the integrity of our own cultures. The stories rooted in experience become beads to trade. It is the story, always the story, that precedes and follows the journey.

Just when you believe in your own sense of place, plan on getting lost. It's not your fault—blame it on Coyote. The terror of the country you thought you knew bears gifts of humility. The landscape that makes you vulnerable also makes you strong. This is the bedrock of southern Utah's beauty: its chameleon nature according to light and weather and season encourages us to make peace with our own contradictory nature. The trickster quality of the canyons is Coyote's cachet.

When the Navajo speak of Coyote, they do so hesitantly, looking over their shoulders, checking the time of year so they won't be heard. They know his stories are told only after the first frost and never after the last thaw. Their culture has been informed by Coyote. He is profane and sacred, a bumbler and a hero. He straddles the canyon walls with wild oats in his belly. And they know him by name—*Ma'ii,* the one never to be taken for granted. They understand his fickle nature, how he seduces fools into believing their own myths, that they matter to the life of the desert.

Coyote knows we do not matter. He knows rocks care nothing for those who wander through them; yet he also knows that those same individuals who care for the rocks will find openings—large openings—that become passageways into the unseen world, where music is heard through doves' wings and wisdom is gleaned from the tails of lizards. Coyote is always nearby but remains hidden. He is an ally because he cares enough to stay wary. He teaches us how to survive.

It is Coyote who wanders naked in the desert and leaves his skin on the highway, allowing us to believe he is dead. He knows sunburned flesh is better than a tanned hide, that days spent in the desert are days soaking up strength. He can retrieve his coat and fluff up his fur after a wild day in the wilderness and meet any man, woman, or child on the streets of Moab and seduce them for dinner. Coyote knows it is the proportion of days spent in wildness that counts in urbane savvy.

Coyote's howl above the canyon says the desert may not depend on his life, but his life depends on the desert.

We would do well to listen.

The canyons of southern Utah are giving birth to a Coyote Clan—hundreds, maybe even thousands, of individuals who are quietly subversive on behalf of the land.

And they are infiltrating our neighborhoods in the most respectable ways, with their long, bushy tails tucked discreetly inside their pants or beneath their skirts.

Members of the Clan are not easily identified, but there are clues. You can see it in their eyes. They are joyful and they are fierce. They can cry louder and laugh harder than anyone on the planet. And they have enormous range.

The Coyote Clan is a raucous bunch: they have drunk from desert potholes and belched forth toads. They tell stories with such virtuosity that you'll swear you have been in the presence of preachers.

The Coyote Clan is also serene. They can float on their backs down the length of any river or lose entire afternoons in the contemplation of stone.

Members of the Clan court risk and will dance on slickrock as flash floods erode the ground beneath their feet. It doesn't matter. They understand the earth re-creates itself day after day.

The images and stories that follow come from Coyote's Canyon. They are dedicated to the Clan, to give them strength when they are away from the slickrock, to jar their memories that beauty is not found in the excessive but in what is lean and spare and subtle.

LION EYES

It was going to be a long ride home for fifteen Navajo children. Dropping kids off five, ten, and twenty miles apart is no small task. We were committed for the night. The sun had just vanished behind Giant's Knuckles, causing those in the back of the pickup to huddle close.

"It gets cold in the desert," I said.

"It's winter," one of the children replied. They covered their mouths with their hands, giggling, as we continued to bump along the dirt roads surrounding Montezuma Creek. What did the driver and I know? We were Anglos.

We had been down by the river for the afternoon. A thin veneer of ice had coalesced along its edge, and the children, bending down, would break off pieces and hold them between their thumbs and forefingers. Before the ice would melt, some brought the thin sheet to their eyes as a lens, while others placed it in their mouths and sucked on the river. Still others winged the ice sheets across the cobbles, watching, listening to them shatter like glass.

Life on the river's edge was explored through whirligig beetles, water skaters, and caddis fly larvae under stones. Canada geese flew above the channel, landing for brief intervals, then continuing on their way. The children followed tracks, expecting to meet a pack of stray dogs hiding in the tamarisks. Our shadows grew longer with the last light of day reflecting on river rapids and willows.

The hours by the river were well spent. Now, in the back of the pickup, the children told tales of days when a horse could enter a hogan and leave as a man; of skinwalkers disguised as coyotes who stalk the reservation with bones in their hands, scratching white crosses on the doors of ill-fated households. They spoke of white owls, ghostly flashes of light that could turn the blood of mice into milk.

Just then, my friend hit the brakes and those of us in the back fell forward.

"What was that?" The driver leaned his head out the window so we could hear him. "Did you see that?"

"What?" we all asked.

"A mountain lion! It streaked across the road. I'll swear it was all tail!"

The children whispered among themselves, "Mountain Lion . . ."

We filed out of the truck. My friend and I walked a few

feet ahead. We found the tracks. A rosette. Five-toed pads, clawless, imprinted on the sand in spite of the cold.

"No question," I said. "Lion. I wonder where she is now?"

Looking into the darkness, I could only imagine the desert cat staring back at us. I looked at the children; most of them were leaning against the truck as headlights approached.

"What's going on?" a local Navajo asked as he rolled down the window of his pickup, his motor idling.

My friend recognized him as the uncle of one of the children. "We think we saw a mountain lion," he said.

"Where? How long ago?"

The other man in the cab of the truck asked if we were sure.

"Pretty sure," I said. "Look at these tracks."

The men got out of their vehicle and shined their flashlights on the ground until they picked up the prints. One of the men knelt down and touched them.

"This is not good," the uncle said. "They kill our sheep." He looked into the night and then back at us. "What color of eyes did it have?"

My friend and I looked at each other. The Navajo elder began reciting the color of animals' eyes at night.

"Deer's eyes are blue. Coyote's eyes are red." His nephew interrupted him. "Green—the lion's eyes were green."

The two men said they would be back with their guns and sons tomorrow.

We returned to the truck, the driver with a handful of kids up front and the rest in the back around me as we nestled together under blankets. The children became un- usually quiet, speaking in low, serious voices about why mountain lions are considered dangerous.

"It's more than just killing sheep," one child explained. "Mountain Lion is a god, one of the supernaturals that has power over us."

Each child gave away little bits of knowledge concern- ing the lion: that it chirps like a bird to fool you; that parts of its body are used for medicine; that in the old days hunters used the sinew of lion for their bows. The children grew more and more anxious as fear seized their voices like two hands around their throats. They were hushed.

We traveled through the starlit desert in silence, except for the hum of the motor and four wheels flying over the washboard.

In time, from the rear of the pickup, came a slow, delib- erate chant. Navajo words—gentle, deep meanderings of music born out of healing. I could not tell who had in- itiated the song, but one by one each child entered the melody. Over and over they sang the same monotonous notes, dreamlike at first, until gradually the cadence quick- ened. The children's mood began to lighten and they swayed back and forth. What had begun as a cautious, fearful tone emerged as a joyous one. Their elders had taught them well. They had sung themselves back to *hózhó,* where the world is balanced and whole.

After the last child had been taken home, my friend and I were left with each other, but the echo of the children's chant remained. With many miles to go, we rolled down the windows in the cab of the truck letting the chilled air blow through. Mountain Lion, whose eyes I did not see, lay on the mesa, her whiskers retrieving each note carried by the wind.

THE BOWL

There was a woman who left the city, her family, her children, left everything behind to retrieve her soul. She came to the desert after seeing her gaunt face in the mirror, the pallor that comes when everything is going out and nothing is coming in. She had noticed for the first time the furrows under her eyes that had been eroded by tears. She did not know the woman in the mirror. She took off her apron, folded it neatly in the drawer, left a note for her family, and closed the door behind her. She knew that her life and the lives of those she loved depended on it.

The woman returned to the place of her childhood, where she last remembered her true nature. She returned to the intimacy of a small canyon that for years had loomed large in her imagination, and there she set up camp. The walls were as she had recalled them, tall and streaked from rim to floor. The rock appeared as draped fabric as she placed her hand flat against its face. The wall was cold; the sun had not yet reached the wash. She began wading the shallow stream that ran down the center of the canyon and chose not to be encumbered by anything. She shed her clothing, took out her hairpins, and squeezed the last lemon she had over her body. Running her hands over her breasts and throat and behind her neck, the woman shivered over her own bravery. This is how it should be, she thought. She was free and frightened and beautiful.

For days the woman wandered in and out of the slickrock maze. She drank from springs and ate the purple fruit of prickly pears. Her needs were met simply. Because she could not see herself, she was unaware of the changes —how her skin became taut and tan, the way in which her hair relaxed and curled itself. She even seemed to walk differently as her toes spread and gripped the sand.

All along the wash, clay balls had been thrown by a raging river. The woman picked one up, pulled off the pebbles until she had a mound of supple clay. She kneaded it as she walked, rubbed the clay between the palms of her hands, and watched it lengthen. She finally sat down on the moist sand and, with her fingers, continued moving up the string of clay. And then she began to coil it, around and around, pinching shut each rotation. She created a bowl.

The woman found other clay balls and put them inside the bowl. She had an idea of making dolls for her children, small clay figurines that she would let dry in the sun. Once again she stopped walking and sat in the sand to work. She split each clay ball in two, which meant she had six small pieces to mold out of three balls she had found. One by one, tiny shapes took form. A girl with open arms above her head; three boys—one standing, one sitting, and one lying down (he was growing, she mused); and then a man and woman facing each other. She had re-created her family. With the few scraps left over she made desert animals: a lizard, a small bird, and a miniature coyote sitting on his haunches. The woman smiled as she looked over her menagerie. She clapped her hands to remove the dried clay and half expected to see them dance. Instead, it began to rain.

Within minutes, the wash began to swell. The woman put the clay creatures into the bowl and sought higher ground up a side canyon, where she found shelter under a large overhang. She was prepared to watch if a flash flood came. And it did. The clear water turned muddy as it began to rise, carrying with it the force of wild horses running with a thunderstorm behind them. The small stream, now a river, rose higher still, gouging into the sandy banks, hurling rocks, roots, and trees downstream. The woman wondered about the animals as she heard stirrings in the grasses and surmised they must be seeking refuge in the side canyons as she was—watching as she was. She pulled her legs in and wrapped her arms around her shins, resting her cheekbones against her knees. She closed her eyes and concentrated on the sound of water bursting through the silence of the canyon.

The roar of the flood gradually softened until it was replaced by birdsong. Swifts and swallows plucked the water for insects while frogs announced their return. The woman raised her head. With the bowl in both hands, she tried to get up but slipped down the hillside, scraping the backs of her thighs on rabbitbrush and sage. She finally reached the wash with the bowl and its contents intact. And then she found herself with another problem: she sank up to her knees in the wet red clay, only to find that the more she tried to pull one foot free, the deeper she sank with the other. Finally, letting go of her struggle, she put the bowl and her family aside, and wallowed in it. She fell sideways and rolled onto her stomach, then over onto her back. She was covered in slimy wet clay and it was delicious. She stretched her hands above her head, flexed her calves, and pointed her toes. The woman laughed hysterically until she became aware of her own echo.

Her body contracted.

She must get control of herself, she thought; what would her husband think. What kind of example was she setting for her children. And then she remembered—she was alone. She sat up and stared at the coiled bowl full of clay people. The woman took out the figurines and planted them in the wash. She placed the animals around them.

"They're on their own," she said out loud. And she walked back to the spring where she had drunk, filled up her bowl with water, and bathed.

The next morning, when the woman awoke, she noticed that the cottonwood branches swaying above her head had sprouted leaves.

She could go home now.

BURIED POEMS

There is a man in Boulder, Utah, who buries poems in the desert. He is an archaeologist who knows through his profession that eventually his words will be excavated, that although they may not be understood now by his community, at a later date his poetry will be held as an artifact, mulled over by minds that will follow his.

This man is alone, walled in by the wilderness he loves and neighbors who don't understand him. They say he spends too much time with the dead, that his loyalties are to bones, that the land could be better used for the planting of corn than the digging of corpses. They say he talks too little and thinks too much for a town like Boulder.

He has lived among the locals for decades, but he is still an outsider. It is the Anasazi who keep him here. They are his neighbors, the ones who court his imagination. It is their echoes reverberating through the canyons that hold him.

He listens and he studies. He pores over the artifacts that come into the museum where he works. When no one is around, he pulls out his glasses, slips on his white cotton gloves, and carefully turns the objects over and over as though some wisdom might speak to him from a sandal or basket or cradle board.

Occasionally, a local or two drop in. He invites them outdoors and encourages them to sit between sage. He takes his hand and sweeps it across the valley and tells them this site was once occupied by over two hundred individuals, continuously from A.D. 1050 to 1200, that this is twice the population living in Boulder today. He tells them the Anasazi were both farmers and hunters and gatherers —planting beans, squash, and corn as they supplemented their diet with big game and rodents. He tries to convince them that the Anasazi, through their technology of manos, metates, pinched pots, and atlatls, were remarkable people well adapted to an inhospitable environment. And then he stops himself, realizing how carried away he has become. He lets the visitors wander among the ruins.

On another day some neighbors ask, "Are you finding anything good out there?"

"It's all good," the archaeologist replies, "corn cobs, charcoal, and chipping debris . . ."

The neighbors are unimpressed. He gives in.

"But one time we were excavating in a particular site and uncovered three ollas—corrugated vessels used for carrying water. Next to these pots were two large balls of clay that had been kneaded. You could still see palm marks from the anonymous hands that had made them. Beneath the pots and clay balls was a burial, the delicate placement of female bones."

He pauses as he rubs his hand over the soil. "I honestly believe she was a potter. We have found no reference to anything like it in the literature. It is most unusual."

The locals look at him, puzzled, and shake their heads. It doesn't register. He sees it in their eyes. They ask him for evidence, and he says they buried it for another generation to uncover. They look at the dry land and they look at him, and they walk away.

The man leaves the museum for the day, locks the door behind him, and retreats to his spot in the rocks. He pulls out his pencil and spiral notebook from a front pocket of his cowboy shirt and begins writing. Poems come to him like wild horses to water. He writes a few lines, tears the paper, and burns the edges with his lighter. He writes another verse, tears it from his notebook, antiques it with fire, and places it in a pile that he holds down with his boot. By the end of the afternoon he has a dozen or more poems. On his way home he buries them.

The man knows the ways of these people. They ranch and they farm. They know the contours of the land, and if a white triangle of paper is sprouting where corn should be, they'll pull it up. Or if the cows are out grazing and happen to kick a sheet of paper into the air, it will be read by the wranglers. And when women are planting borders of zinnias around their homes and uncover a poem with their trowel, they'll call their neighbors just to pass the words along.

Which is exactly what happened. Within a matter of days the whole town of Boulder, Utah, was reading poetry to one another.

Some think they are love poems written by an Indian. Others guess they are clues to a buried treasure left by John Wesley Powell or Father Escalante. And still others believe they are personal messages left especially for them by a deceased family member, which is how they became known as "the ghost poems."

The archaeologist listens. He walks about town with his hands in his pockets. People are talking across fences, over melon stands, and inside their automobiles. Some individuals are even offering to buy them from their friends. But the finders of the poems won't sell. The man who buries the poems quietly slips into the convenience store and buys another notebook and lighter and returns to his place in the rocks.

His poems become shorter, more cryptic, until finally they are a series of pictographs—the pictographs found in Calf Creek Canyon, Coyote Gulch, and Mimi's Grotto.

The town eventually seeks him out, asking if he knows what these picture poems might mean. He refers them to different canyons, invites them to his slide shows, and tells them stories about the Anasazi who once lived where they do now. He explains how these drawings on canyon walls are a reflection of Anasazi culture, of rituals, and all that mattered in their lives. Now, he tells them, we can only speculate. The townsfolk are listening. He sees it in their eyes.

A local hands him a poem and says, "Read this. My boy found it buried near the overhang behind our ranch."

The archaeologist reads the poem out loud:

SOUNDS

The ruin clings to the cliff
Under the arching sandstone.
It is quiet now.
No longer do you hear the laughter,
The everyday sounds:
Women making pottery—the slap, slap of clay,
People cooking,
Men returning from the hunt,
The builders,
Children playing,
The cries of sorrow when a loved one passes on.
They are gone now—
The Anasazi.

The survivors.
The adapters.
The only sounds now
Are those of the wind
The raucous sound of the raven,
The descending sound of the canyon wren.
The guardians.

Poem by Larry Davis,
an archaeologist in Boulder, Utah

By now, the town of Boulder has hundreds of these poems in its possession. They hang in the schoolhouse, where the children are taking up the mystery. The community still wonders who is responsible for these writings, questioning just how long they will continue to be found. But poems keep appearing in the strangest places: in milk cans, on tractor seats, church pews, and irrigation ditches. And, rumor has it, the canyons are filled with them. The man who buries poems in the desert may turn the whole damned town into archaeologists. The next thing we'll hear is that the locals want to preserve the wilderness for its poetry.

KOKOPELLI'S RETURN

One night, beneath the ruins of Keet Seel, we heard flute music—music so sweet it could have split the seeds of corn. Earlier we had wandered through the rooms of Keet Seel, admiring the redrock construction dabbed into the sandstone alcove like swallows' nests, but there had been no music then, only the silence pressing against us in the cool Anasazi air.

Above the ruins, clouds covered the full face of the moon like gauze. The land seemed to bow with the melody of the flute. I reached for my husband's arm and he reached for our friend. We kept hold of one another like children, and we listened, holding our breaths between the intervals of our own heartbeats. The flute music flowed out from the cliff dwelling like an ancient breath.

The next morning we sat around camp, drinking rose hip tea. We were tired and stiff from the cold, still half stunned from the night before. Our friend, who was Hopi, looked down at the cup he held in both hands and told a story:

A man traveled through this country with a bag of corn seed over one shoulder. His shadow against the desert looked like a deformity. He would stop at every village and teach the people how to plant corn. And then when the sun slipped behind the mesa and the village was asleep, he would walk through the cornfields playing his flute. The seeds would sprout, pushing themselves up through the red, sandy soil, and follow the high-pitched notes upward. The sun would rise and the man would be gone, leaving cornstalks the height of a young girl, shimmering in the morning light. Many of the young women would complain of a fullness in their bellies. The elders would smile, knowing they were pregnant. They would look to the southwest and call him "Kokopelli."

We finished our tea, broke camp, and organized our packs for the trail. Before leaving, I walked back to the base of Keet Seel. The ruins appeared darker than usual, full of shadows that moved from room to room. My eyes followed the tall timbers from floor to ceiling as I imagined macaws perched on top. Kivas held darkness below, and I wondered if old men's bones might be buried there. Just then, in a stream of light, a pictograph on the ceiling of the alcove jumped out. It was a buglike creature, but as I focused more clearly, I recognized it as the humpbacked flute player.

"Kokopelli," I whispered to myself. "It must be Kokopelli."

The light shifted and he seemed to be rocking on his back. I had missed him the day before, noticing only the pictographs of bighorn sheep and spirals. At that moment, I recalled the flute music that flooded the canyon the night before and the clouds like gossamer hands with long, long fingers that pulled me into an abyss of sleep. I placed my hand over my stomach, turned away from the ruins, and walked back toward my fellow campers. Halfway down the canyon, I felt stirrings in my belly. Sweet corn was sprouting all along the river.

PERFECT KIVA

In a poorly lit corner of a restaurant in Moab, a woman draws a map on a napkin and slips it to a man. The man studies the paper square carefully and asks her a few questions. He thanks her. They pay for their meals and then part ways.

The man stops at a gas station, fills up his truck, then walks to the corner pay phone and makes three calls. Within hours, he meets five friends in Blanding, Utah, at the Rainbow Café. They conspire under plastic jade lanterns, eating Navajo tacos and egg rolls.

"It's called Perfect Kiva. We'll camp on top of the mesa tonight, then hike into the canyon tomorrow. The site is on our right, up high, the third ledge down. I have the map."

The six left Blanding in three trucks. The man with the map led them in the dark across miles of dirt roads that crisscrossed the mesa. In a sense, he had blindfolded them. That was his plan, and his promise to the woman in Moab.

Their camp appeared as a black hole in the desert. Each person drew out his flashlight and checked the ground for cowpies and scorpions. One by one, they threw down their sleeping bags and fell asleep. Dream time was kept by the rotation of stars.

Dawn came into the country like a secret. The six had burrowed so deep inside their bags that they emerged like startled ground squirrels after an eight-hour hibernation. The black hole of the previous night had been transformed into a bevy of piñon and juniper. A few yards beyond was a cut in the desert a quarter mile wide.

Camp was erased. Cars were locked. Water bottles were filled and packs put on. The pace was brisk as they descended into one of the finger canyons. For two hours they walked in and out of morning shadows, until, finally, they stood on the slickrock in full sunlight.

The man with the map studied the cliffs, looking for the perfect alcove with the perfect kiva. Placing their trust in the leader, the others kept walking and found pleasures in small things like blister beetles and feathers snatched from the air by sage. The desert heat loosened the muscles and spirit of the group. Joy crept in and filled their boots.

A few ran up and down boulders just to see if their courage could hold them. Others focused on birds—a lazuli bunting here, an ash-throated flycatcher there. But the man with the map kept looking.

A raven flew out from the rocks.

"There it is!" cried the leader. "The third ledge down. I'll bet that's our alcove."

The six began to climb where the raven flew. They hiked straight up, some on hands and knees, through the sandstone scree, until finally, breathless, they encountered the ruins. Upright and stable, in spite of the thousand feet below them, the friends stood in wonder. They had entered an open-sided hallway of stone. Pink stone. Stone so soft that if held it would crumble.

There were figures with broad shoulders and wild eyes staring at them from inside the rock—petroglyphs that not only seized the imagination but turned it upside down. Animals with bear bodies and deer heads danced on the overhang. Walls made of dry-laid stones divided the ledge. Most of them had tumbled with time: no mortar had been used, just the careful placement of stone against stone to house the Anasazi.

Beyond the walls were mealing bins, standing stones that corralled the corn. The manos and metates were gone, but images of women chanting corn to meal were as real as the shriveled cobs piled inside the granary.

Perfect Kiva was more subtle. It was recognizable only by the fraying juniper bark that had shown through the eroded sand. The six sat outside the circle until calm. The kiva seemed to ask that of them. Five slabs of sandstone framed the entrance, which appeared as a dark square on the ledge floor. A juniper ladder with rungs of willow led to the underworld. They paused. The ladder that had supported the Ancient Ones might not support them. They chose not to use it. Instead, they jury-rigged a sling out of nylon cording and carabiners and anchored it around a boulder. They moved the ladder aside and, one by one, lowered themselves into the kiva. Perfect Kiva—round like Earth. Hidden in the earth, the six sat.

It took a few minutes for their eyes to adjust. Cobwebs dangled from the wooden ceiling, most likely black widows spinning webs off the cribbed logs and pilasters. Walls bricked, then plastered, created the smooth red circumference of the ceremonial chamber. Four shelves were cut into the walls. Each was lined with juniper lace and berries. Two full moons, one green and one white, faced each other on the east and west walls. A green serpent of the same pigment moved on the north wall, west to east, connecting the circles.

No one spoke.

The six remained captive to their own meanderings, each individual absorbing what he was in need of. An angle of light poured through the hole in the ceiling as the dust in the air danced up the ladder. They breathed deeply. It was old, old air.

The longer they sat in the kiva, the more they saw. There was a hearth in the center, a smoke vent to the south, eight loom anchors, and the fine desert powder they were sitting on. But the focus inside the kiva was on the *sipapu*— the small hole in the floor that, according to the Hopi, promises emergence. In time, each one circled the *sipapu* with his fingers and raised himself on the slings. They untied the rope from around the boulder and placed the Anasazi ladder back where it had been for as long as ravens had a memory.

A few months later, in a poorly lit corner of a restaurant in Moab, a woman speaks softly to a man.

"They took the ladder, put it in a museum, and stabilized the kiva. It's just not the same," she whispers. "They fear aging and want it stopped like an insect in amber."

He studies her face and asks her a few questions. He thanks her. They pay for their meals and then part ways.

The man stops at a gas station, fills up his truck, then walks to the corner pay phone and makes three calls. Within hours the six meet in Blanding at the Rainbow Café.

"It's called theft in the name of preservation," he says. "The ladder is held hostage at the local museum. It belongs to the desert. It must be returned."

The friends move closer around the table.

"Tomorrow—" he says.

"Tonight," they insist.

Dawn came into the country like a secret.

A WOMAN'S DANCE

She came to the desert to dance. The woman gathered a variety of plants: mullein, sage, chamisa, mint, Oregon grape, aster, equisetum, and yarrow. She carried them in the folds of her long red skirt to a clearing. It was a meadow defined by juniper. She placed the plants in the center and returned to the trees. She took off the paisley bandanna wrapped around her forehead and knelt on the red sand.

"Good death," she said, as her hands sifted the wood dust of a decaying tree. She opened her scarf and placed the henna wood chips on the silk square. After she had gathered enough for the task, she brought the four corners together, tied them, and walked back to the clearing. She was not alone. Flickers, robins, magpies, and jays accompanied her. The woman carefully untied one of the corners and let the wood dust sprinkle to the ground as she walked in a circle. Next, she retrieved the plants from the center and arranged them end to end on top of the wood dust to define her circle more clearly. She liked what she saw.

Movement surrounded her. The wind, clouds, grasses, and birds—all reminded her that nothing stands still. She held up the hem of her skirt in both hands and began walking briskly around the circle. Deep breaths took the aroma of mint and sage down to her toes. Her long, spirited stride broke into short leaps with extended arms as she entered the circle dancing, without guile, without notice, without any thought of herself. She danced from the joy of all she was a part of.

Pronghorn Antelope entered the circle through her body. She danced Eagle, Raven, and Bear. The Four Seasons sent her swirling as she danced to ignite the Moon. She danced until gravity pulled her down, and then she rested, her eyes closed, with nothing moving but her heart and lungs, beating, breathing, against the hot, dry desert.

With her ear against the earth, the woman listened. A chant began to rise. Slowly she raised her body like a lizard. An audience had gathered. Each individual sat crosslegged around the plant circle with a found instrument: rocks, bones, sticks, stumps, whistles, and voices. For hours they played music, organic and whole, as she danced. Her hands, like serpents, encouraged primal sounds as she arched forward and back with the grasses. She was the wind that inspired change. They were a tribe creating a landscape where lines between the real and imagined were thinly drawn.

The light deepened, shadows lengthened, and the woman began to turn. Her turns widened with each rotation until she stopped, perfectly balanced. The woman stepped outside the circle and kissed the palms of her hands and placed them on the earth.

The dance was over.

The audience rose, refreshed. Each picked up one of the plants that held the circle and took a handful of wood dust to scatter, leaving no clues in the clearing of ever having been there. They disappeared as mysteriously as they had arrived.

And the woman who came to the desert to dance simply ran her fingers through her long black hair and smiled.

THE STONE SPIRAL

They gathered stones along the river. Dark to light. It was a game at first, something to move along a slow afternoon. But once they began to see all the colors of the riverbed, the spectrum of stones became an obsession. Blacks were easy, so were whites. Shades of red were plentiful—after all, they were the sandstone that made up the country. Green stones shattered from limestone appeared foreign and exotic, as did lavenders and blues from slate and shale. Brown and yellow stones were harder to find—the sulphur and quartz most people take for granted. They piled the rocks on the sand like a stash of old billiard balls.

After the various hues had been selected in all their gradations, the man and the woman began to create a spiral. Together they lifted a large, black river cobble and placed it in the center. It was smooth and polished and elegant. Next to the black stone was a not-so-black stone, five stones down a charcoal one, next to it, deep purple. Then came the blue stones: navy, cobalt, teal, and turquoise. An olive stone carried the spectrum to yellow, orange, red-orange, maroon, indigo, lavender, pale pink, and white. The spiral wound around the floodplain like a coiled snake.

After the spiral was complete, they walked around it (some adjustments were made), talking themselves through each stone and color. They began to tell stories about the creation of the world, how this stone ruled the sky and this stone ruled the forest and this one the sea. They picked guardian stones for animals and birds, insects, and spiders. The black center stone became Black Widow's domain. They imagined her underneath, spinning the web, binding them all together.

The light began to change. The temperature seemed to drop, and the river was slowing down as if the mountain snows had given enough of themselves that day. The sun was disappearing behind a mesa. Reflected light bouncing off canyon walls intensified the colors until even human skin appeared burnished and bronzed.

Welcoming twilight, the couple began hurling small white pebbles into the sky, ducking at first so they wouldn't be hit, and then laughing, crying out loud, "first star, second star, third star, fourth . . ." And then another game ensued. They found themselves lying on the riverbank counting stars. It surprised them how long it really took for the night sky to be lit. An hour after sunset only one hundred stars had appeared. But as the man and the woman turned to each other, the stars began to double and triple exponentially, until the Milky Way draped over them. By this time, the lovers drifted in and out of sleep until dawn.

When they awoke, the stars were gone. They found themselves covered with leaves. But their stone spiral was still intact. The stones were pale. The man and woman pretended the stones were thirsty, and walked down to the river. With cupped hands they returned to the rocks with water; again and again, they let the stones drink. They seemed to blush and gurgle and shine. The spectrum of colored stones was revived.

The sun moved to midsky as the couple sat among the stones and spoke of family. With willow sticks they wrote the names of mothers, fathers, brothers, sisters, cousins, aunts and uncles, grandmothers and grandfathers in the soft sand outside the spiral. They flirted with each other, saying between the two of them their relatives could fill the desert. Standing up, they recognized what extraordinary clans they belonged to.

With no more thought than a flock of birds gives to flight, the man and woman leaped from stone to stone. Taking hold of one another's hands, with great joy, they entered the current and floated like a wish downriver.

RED

Red, Vico told me one day, is the colour of sacrifice.

Really?

Both pain and triumph, he said, are in the colour red, and of course, blood.

—John Berger,
King

AMERICA'S REDROCK WILDERNESS

Wilderness is not a belief. It is a place. And in Utah, we know these places by name:

Little Goose Creek
Newfoundland Mountains
Silver Island Mountains
Cedar Mountains
Stansbury Mountains
North Stansbury
Big Hollow
Deep Creek Mountains
Fish Springs Range
Dugway Mountains
Rockwell
House Range
Swasey Mountain

Notch Peak
Howell Peak
Conger Mountain
King Top
Wah Wah Mountains
Granite Peak
White Rock Range
Cougar Canyon–Doc's Pass
Beaver Dam Slope
Joshua Tree
Beaver Dam Wash
Red Mountain
Cottonwood Creek
Greater Zion
Canaan Mountain
Parunuweap Canyon
The Watchman
North Fork Virgin River
Orderville Canyon
Deep Creek
Goose Creek
Red Butte
LaVerkin Creek Canyon
Spring Creek Canyon
Taylor Creek Canyon
Beartrap Canyon
Black Ridge

Moquith Mountain
Upper Kanab Creek
Grand Staircase
Paria-Hackberry
Squaw and Willis Canyon
East of Bryce
Box Canyon
The Blues
Mud Spring Canyon
The Cockscomb
Kaiparowits Plateau
Wahweap–Paradise Canyon
Nipple Bench
Warm Creek
Squak Canyon
Burning Hills
Fiftymile Mountain
Fiftymile Bench
Cave Point
Carcass Canyon
Horse Spring Canyon
Escalante Canyons
Little Egypt
Scorpian
Hurricane Wash
Fortymile Gulch
Phipps-Death Hollow

Steep Creek
Lampstand
Studhorse Peaks
Colt Mesa Long Canyon
Notom Bench
Dogwater Creek
Fremont Gorge
Henry Mountains
Mount Ellen–Blue Hills
Bull Mountain
Ragged Mountain
Mount Pennell
Bullfrog Creek
Mount Hillers
Dirty Devil
Fiddler Butte
White Canyon
Cheesebox Canyon
Harmony Flat
Gravel Canyon
Fortknocker Canyon
Glen Canyon
Mancos Mesa
Little Rockies
San Juan–Anasazi
Nokai Dome
Grand Gulch

Pine Canyon

Bullet Canyon

Sheiks Canyon

Slickhorn Canyon

Fish and Owl Creek Canyons

Road Canyon

San Juan River

Comb Ridge

Arch and Mule Canyons

Squaw & Cross Canyons

Dark Canyon

Sheep Canyon

Canyonlands Basin

Shafer Canyon

Gooseneck

Indian Creek

Harts Point

Bridger Jack Mesa

Butler Wash

Behind the Rocks

Goldbar Canyon

Hunters Canyon

Hatch Wash

LaSal Canyons

Mill Creek Canyon

Negro Bill Canyon

Mary Jane Canyon

Fisher Towers

Sewemup Mesa

Beaver Creek

Granite Creek

Westwater Canyon

Black Ridge Canyons

Arches–Lost Spring Canyon

Labyrinth Canyon

Upper Horseshoe Canyon

San Rafael Swell

Sid's Mountain

Mexican Mountain

San Rafael Reef

Wild Horse Mesa

Muddy Creek

Crack Canyon

Cistern Canyon

Chute Canyon

Hondu Country

Devil's Canyon

Upper Muddy Creek

Cedar Mountain

Mussentuchit Badlands

Red Desert

Limestone Cliffs

Jones Bench

Books Cliffs–Desolation Canyon

Jack Canyon

Floy Canyon

Nine-Mile Canyon

Turtle Canyon

Coal Canyon

Spruce Canyon

Flume Canyon

White River

Greater Dinosaur

Daniel's Canyon

Moonshine Draw

Bull Canyon

Wild Mountain

Diamond Breaks

Cold Springs Mountain

Mount Naomi

Wellsville Mountains

High Uintas

Mount Olympus

Twin Peaks

Lone Peak

Mount Timpanogos

Mount Nebo

Pine Valley Mountains

Ashdown Gorge

Box-Death Hollow

Dark-Woodenshoe Canyon

Beaver Dam Mountains
Paria Canyon–Vermillion Cliffs
Moon-Eyed Horse Canyon

What do these places have to say to us as human beings at this point in time? What do they have to say about life during the Cretaceous, Jurassic, and Triassic eras? What do they have to say to us about the erosion and uplift of our souls and imaginations?

What voices are being carried inside the canyons by the salamanders, toads, and tree frogs? Or the species of turtles, lizards, and snakes who are also living on the Colorado Plateau?

A rattlesnake coiled and hissing is exposed on the slick-rock.

Think about the hundreds of species of birds and mammals on the plateau: white-throated swifts, violet-green swallows, ravens, coyote, mountain lion, and mule deer. We may see them, we may not. Always, they are watching. Turkey vultures are watching.

And what kind of standing do the hundreds of species of plants have in the desert, especially forty-two threatened species, the sand poppy among them?

There are songs still being sung and stories that long to be told in the places where people lived thousands of years ago, places that braid the Colorado Plateau together. In so many ways, the Anasazi have never left. Handprints on redrock walls. Anasazi applause.

These wildlands are alive. When one of us says, "Look, there's nothing out there," what we are really saying is, "*I cannot see.*"

The Colorado Plateau is wild. There is still wilderness here, big wilderness. Wilderness holds an original presence giving expression to that which we lack, the losses we long to recover, the absences we seek to fill. Wilderness revives the memory of unity. Through its protection, we can find faith in our humanity.

We have a history in this country of environmental courage, and its roots are found in direct contact with the beauty of the natural world that sustains us. The sacred heart of this continent beats in the unagitated and free landscapes of North America.

Wallace Stegner writes in *Beyond the Hundredth Meridian* of "A Blueprint for a Dryland Democracy," referring to John Wesley Powell's 1877 "Arid Lands Report." Powell's report was, in Stegner's words, "a complete revolution in the system of land surveys, land policy, land tenure . . . in the West, and a denial of almost every cherished fantasy and myth associated with Western migration and the American Dream . . ."

Almost 120 years later, these arid lands are still inspiring a revolution of thought. Public lands within the

Colorado Plateau possess spiritual values that cannot be measured in economic terms. They dare us to think in geologic terms: Kayenta, Moenavi, Chinle, Shinarump, Toroweep, Coconino, and Supai. We are absorbed into a rich, vibrant narrative of vertical time and horizontal space.

We can learn something from this redrock country as we stand on its edge, looking in. We can learn humility in the face of Creation, reverence in the presence of God, and faith in one another for exercising restraint in the name of what lands should be developed and what lands should be preserved.

This country's wisdom still resides in its populace, in the pragmatic and generous spirits of everyday citizens who have not forgotten their kinship with nature. They are individuals who will forever hold the standard of the wild high, knowing in their hearts that natural engagement is not an interlude but a daily practice, a commitment each generation must renew in the name of the land. If we listen to our politicians we must ask some serious questions. Who is speaking on the side of time? *Deep time.* And who is considering the soulful existence of other creatures?

What we have witnessed in the ongoing struggle to protect America's Redrock Wilderness is that responsive citizenship matters. Individual voices are heard, and when collectively spoken they reverberate on canyon walls. This passion for the wild endures and can lead to social change long after a specific piece of legislation has been forgotten.

The Hopi Elders have told us, it is time for healing. A healing must begin within our communities, within ourselves, regarding our relationship to the Earth, Wild Earth.

we are in the process of

        becoming Earth.

We are not separate.
We belong to a much larger community than we know.
We are here because of love.

        ringing

    this   silence

This silence—   —is the bedrock of

   our   democracy.

STATEMENT

BEFORE THE SENATE SUBCOMMITTEE ON
FOREST & PUBLIC LANDS MANAGEMENT
REGARDING
THE UTAH PUBLIC LANDS MANAGEMENT ACT OF 1995
WASHINGTON, D.C.
JULY 13, 1995

Mr. Chairman, members of this subcommittee, my name is Terry Tempest Williams. I am a native of Utah. My family roots run deep, holding me in place: five, six generations of Mormon stock run through my veins. Our family has made its living on the land for the last six decades laying pipe in the Utah substrate. We are a family of pipeline contractors and although I have never dug the ditches, I love and care for the men who do: my brothers, cousins, uncle, father, John Henry Tempest, my grandfather, John Henry Tempest, Jr., who is in his ninetieth year, even my great-grandfather, John Henry Tempest, Sr. We understand the power of continuity and our debt to these lands that have given us livelihood. As a Utah family, we would like to enter into the Congressional Record personal letters, four generations' worth, of why we care about wilderness, why we do not favor Senate Bill 884, and why we want more wilderness designation in Utah, not less. Some of the letters are forthcoming, some I have brought with me. These letters represent men and women, Republicans and Democrats alike, registered voters and voices too young to vote, but not too young to register their opinions. They are individual and original, some sealed, some open. It is a gesture of sincere concern for what we hold dear.

I appreciate this time to be able to share with you some of my own thoughts about the Utah Public Lands Management Act of 1995.

It is not a wilderness bill that the majority of Utahns recognize, want, or desire.

It is not a wilderness bill that honors or respects our history as a people.

It is not a wilderness bill that honors or respects the natural laws required for a healthy environment.

And it is not a wilderness bill that takes an empathetic stance toward our future.

It is a wilderness bill that lacks vision and undermines the bipartisan principles inherent in the Wilderness Act of 1964.

Quite simply, in the name of political expediency and with eyes capable of seeing only through the lens of economics, our public lands in Utah are being sacrificed. Our congressional delegation has told you that this issue must be resolved now, that this debate over the wildlands in Utah has torn our state in half. But I prefer to take the artist Frederick Sommer's approach when he says, "Quarreling is the cork of a good wish."

What is it we wish for?

In Utah, there was a man with a vision. He dreamed of a civilization bright with lights and strong of belief. He knew the industrious nature of work and picked the beehive as his symbol. He loved the land he saw before him, a landscape so vast, pristine, and virginal, that he recognized it as the kingdom of God, a place for saints with a desire for home. The desert country of the Great Basin and Colorado Plateau was an answer to prayers of spiritual sovereignty.

He sent families north into the mountains and south into the valleys where redrock walls rose upward like praying hands. He said, "We will create Zion among the wilderness." And with great stamina and imagination akin only to communities committed to faith, the building of culture among the pioneers began. Humble ranches, small businesses, and cottage industries of silk and wool sprung up and a United Order was dreamed.

Brigham Young, the colonizing prophet of the Mormons, brought with him not only a religion and a life but a land ethic.

Here are the stupendous works of the God of Nature, though all do not appreciate His wisdom as manifested in his works. . . . I could sit here for a month and reflect on the mercies of God.

Time. Reflection. Mercy. These qualities were not revered as elsewhere in the Utah Public Lands Act of 1995. There is little gratitude extended on behalf of these sacred lands.

Only a few generations ago, Utah was settled on spiritual grounds. It is ironic that now Utah must be protected on spiritual grounds for the generations to come.

What do we wish for?

To be whole. To be complete. Wildness reminds us what it means to be human, what we are connected to rather than what we are separate from. *"Our troubles,"* the Pulitzer Prize–winning scientist Edward O. Wilson writes,

arise from the fact that we do not know what we are and cannot agree on what we want to be. . . . Humanity is part of nature, a species that evolved among other species. The more closely we identify ourselves with the rest of life, the more quickly we will be able to discover the sources of human sensibility and acquire knowledge on which an enduring ethic, a sense of preferred direction, can be built.

Wilderness is both the bedrock lands of southern Utah and a metaphor of "unlimited possibility." The question must be asked, "How can we cut ourselves off from the very source of our creation?"

This is not about economics. This is not about the preservation of ranching culture in America. And it is especially not about settling a political feud once and for all. This is about putting ourselves in accordance with nature, of consecrating these lands by remembering our relationships to them. A strong wilderness bill as recommended by Congressman Maurice Hinchey, HR 1500, is an act of such consecration. At a recent family gathering, my uncle Richard Tempest, a former Republican state senator, said simply, "Wilderness is a feeling."

Mr. Chairman, if you know wilderness in the way you know love, you would be unwilling to let it go. We are talking about the body of the beloved, not real estate. We must ask ourselves as Americans, "Can we really survive the worship of our own destructiveness?" We do not exist in isolation. Our sense of community and compassionate intelligence must be extended to all life-forms, plants, animals, rocks, rivers, and human beings. This is the story of our past and it will be the story of our future.

Senate Bill 884 falls desperately short of these ideals.

Who can say how much nature can be destroyed without consequence? Who can say how much land can be used for extractive purposes until it is rendered barren forever? And who can say what the human spirit will be crying out for one hundred years from now? Two hundred years from now? A few weeks ago, Yosemite National Park had to close its gates and not allow any more visitors entry; the park was overcrowded. Last week, Yellowstone reported traffic gridlocks in the Lamar Valley, carloads of families with the wish of seeing a wolf. Did our country's lawmakers who held the vision of national parks in the nineteenth century dream of this kind of hunger? In the same vein, can you as our lawmakers today, toward the end of the twentieth century, imagine what the sanctity of wilderness in Utah might hold for us as a people at the turn of the twenty-first century?

We must act with this kind of vision and concern not just for ourselves, but for our children and our children's children. This is our natural heritage. And we are desperate for visionary leadership.

It's strange how deserts turn us into believers. I believe in walking in a landscape of mirages because you learn humility. I believe in living in a land of little water because life is drawn together. And I believe in the gathering of bones as a testament to spirits that have moved on.

If the desert is holy, it is because it is a forgotten place that allows us to remember the sacred. Perhaps that is why every pilgrimage to the desert is a pilgrimage to the self. There is no place to hide and so we are found.

Wilderness courts our souls. When I sat in church throughout my growing years, I listened to teachings about Christ walking in the wilderness for forty days and forty nights, reclaiming his strength, where he was able to say to Satan, "Get thee hence." And when I imagined

Joseph Smith kneeling in a grove of trees as he received his vision to create a new religion, I believed their sojourns into nature were sacred. Are ours any less?

There is a Mormon scripture, from the Doctrine and Covenants section 88:44–47, that I carry with me:

> *The earth rolls upon her wings, and the sun giveth his light by day, and the moon giveth her light by night, and the stars also give their light, as they roll upon their wings in their glory, in the midst and power of God.*
>
> *Unto what shall I liken these kingdoms that ye may understand?*
>
> *Behold all these are kingdoms and any man who hath seen any or the least of these hath seen God moving in his majesty and power.*

Without a philosophy of wildness and the recognition of its inherent spiritual values, we will, as E. O. Wilson reminds us, "descend farther from heaven's air if we forget how much the natural world means to us."

For those of us who so love these lands in Utah, who recognize America's Redrock Wilderness as a sanctuary for the preservation of our souls, Senate Bill 884, the Utah Public Lands Management Act of 1995, is the beginning of this forgetting, a forgetting we may never reclaim.

BLOODLINES

There is a woman who is a tailor. She lives in Green River, Utah, and makes her livelihood performing alterations, taking in a few inches here, letting out a few inches there, basting in hems, then finishing them with a feather stitch.

While hiking in the San Rafael Swell, this woman was raped, thrown down face-first on the sand. She never saw the face of her assailant. What she knew was this: in that act of violence she lost her voice. She was unable to cry for help. He left her violated and raw.

The woman returned home and told no one of her experience. Instead, she grabbed a large spool of red thread, a pair of scissors, and returned to the Swell.

The woman cut pieces of thread and placed them delicately on the desert. Six inches. Three inches. Twelve inches. They appeared as a loose stitched seam upon the land. She saw them as bloodlines, remembering the fetishes of Zuni she had held that draw the heart down. She recalled rabbit, lizard, and rattlesnake. She continued to cut lines, from memory, of animals she had known, seen, and spent time with in these redrock canyons: deer, mountain lion, flicker, and raven. And on one occasion she recalled watching a black bear rambling down Crack Canyon. For this creature, she left a line of red thread three feet long. She cut one-inch threads for frogs and left them inside potholes to wriggle in the rain when the basins would inevitably fill.

Time and space shift.

It is fall.

The woman is now walking along the banks of the Colorado River. She takes her spool of red thread, ties one end to a juniper and then begins walking with the river, following each bend, each curve, her red thread trailing behind her for miles, stitching together what she has lost.

It is spring.

The woman is standing in the deep heat of the desert beside a large boulder known by locals as "the birthing rock." Tiny feet the size of her index finger are etched on stone. Ten toes of hope point to figures of women bearing down, legs spread, with the heads of children coming forth. She recognizes them as two beings seen as one, repeatedly.

The woman picks up an obsidian chip that has been worked by ancient hands; the flaked edge is razor sharp. She holds it between her fingers like a pencil, opens her left hand and traces her own lifeline from beginning to end. The crescent moon below her thumb turns red. She places her palm on the boulder and screams.

ZION

One of my earliest memories
is visiting Zion National Park
in the southwestern corner of Utah.
My brothers and I, with our cousins,
were taken there by our mothers.
What I remember is being led
on a steep path to "The Weeping Rock."
Once there, the temperature cooled,
the sun was shielded.
Our eyes adjusted to the darkness.
A tall black wall with ferns dripping
loomed before us—
I don't recall our mothers
offering any explanation.
And I don't think I wondered
why the rock was crying

or what it was weeping for.
I just remember standing there,
as children, our small hands open
receiving the rock's tears.

TO BE TAKEN

*The revolutionary question is: What about the Other? . . .
It is not enough to rail against the descending darkness of bar-
barity . . . One can refuse to play the game. A holding action
can be fought. Alternatives must be kept alive. While learning
the slow art of revolutionary patience.*

— Breyten Breytenbach
"Tortoise Steps"

Tortoise steps.
Slow steps.
Four steps like a tank with a tail dragging in the sand.
Tortoise steps—land-based, landlocked, dusty like the
desert tortoise himself, fenced in, a prisoner on his own
reservation, teaching us the slow art of revolutionary patience.

It is Christmas. We gather in our grandparents' home: aunts, uncles, cousins, babies—four generations wipe their feet at the holiday mat. One by one, we open the front door, "Hello," "We're here," glass panes iced are beginning to melt from the heat of bodies together. Our grandfather Jack, now ninety, presides. His sons, John and Richard, walk in dressed in tweed sport coats and Levi's; their polished boots could kill spiders in corners. My aunt Ruth enters with her arms full of gifts. Jack's sister, Norinne, in her eighties, sits in the living room with her hands folded tightly, greeting each one of us with a formality we have come to expect.

Tradition.

On this night, we know a buffet is prepared: filet mignon, marinated carrots, asparagus, and cauliflower, a cranberry salad, warbread (a recipe our great-grandmother Mamie Comstock Tempest improvised during the Depression when provisions were scarce and raisins plentiful), and the same silver serving piece is obscene with chocolates.

The Christmas tree stands in the center of the room, "the grandchildren's tree," and we remember our grandmother Mimi, the matriarch of this family, whose last Christmas was in 1988. We remember her. We remember all of our dead.

Candles burn. I walk into the dining room, pick up a plate and circle the table.

"What's new, Terrence?" my uncle asks, ribbing me.

"Not a thing, Rich," I respond. We both look up from the buffet smiling.

I take some meat with my fingers. He spears vegetables. We return to the living room and find a seat. The rest of the family gathers. Jack sits in the wing-backed chair, his hands on both armrests. My father sits across the room from his brother.

"So how did the meeting go last week?"

"Terrible," Rich says.

"What did they decide?"

"Simple," my uncle says. "Tortoises are more important than people."

Heads turn, attention fixes on matters of the Tempest Company, the family construction business that began with our great-grandfather in the early part of the century, a company my brothers all work for, cousins, too.

"What are you talking about?" I ask.

"Where have you been?" my father asks incredulously. "We've been shut down eighteen months because of that" —he stops himself in deference to his aunt—"that *stupid* Endangered Species Act."

I look at my brother Steve who nods his head as he looks at our cousin Bob who looks at his sister Lynne who shakes her head as she turns to Brooke.

"I attended the public meeting where they discussed the Habitat Management Plan," Rich says to us.

"And?" Lynne asks as she walks over to her father and offers him a piece of warbread.

"They ruled in favor of the tortoise."

"Which job is this, John?" asks Brooke, who at the time was working for the governor's office of budget and planning as the liaison between environmental groups and the state.

"It's the last leg of the Information Highway," Dad says. "Seven miles of fiber optic cable running from the town of Hurricane to St. George linking rural Utah to the Wasatch Front."

"We're held up in permits," Rich explains. "A construction permit won't be issued until U.S. West complies with federal agencies."

"The government's gone too far," my great-aunt interjects.

"Too far?" My father says, his voice rising like water ready to boil. "Too far? We've had to hire a full-time biologist at sixty dollars an hour who does nothing but look for these imaginary animals. Every day he circles the crew singing the same song, 'Nope, haven't seen one yet.' "

"The guy's from BYU and sits in the cab of his truck most of the day reading scriptures," adds Steve, who is the superintendent.

"Thou shall not kill a turtle," someone mutters under his breath.

"Sixty bucks an hour," Dad reiterates. "That's twice as

much as our foremen make! It would be cheaper to buy a poolside condominium for each mating pair of tortoises than to adhere to the costs of this ridiculous Act."

"The government's gone too far," my aunt restates like a delayed echo.

"And on top of that we have to conduct a 'turtle training course—' "

"Tortoise, John," his granddaughter Callie interrupts. I wink at my niece.

"A turtle training course for our men, *our men,* so they can learn to identify one and then remember to check under the tires and skids for tortoises looking for shade before turning on the backhoes after lunch."

Rich stands up to get some more food.

"One hundred thousand dollars if we run over one," he says, making himself a sandwich.

"Is that worth a hundred grand?" my father snaps.

"From the tortoise's point of view . . ." Lynne says, pushing.

"What's St. George now, the fourth fastest growing community in the country?" Brooke asks.

"Not if the enviros have anything to do with it," Rich says.

"What do you kids want? To stop progress? You and your environmentalist friends have lost all credibility. One local told us, a bunch of radicals actually planted a tortoise in the parking lot of the Wal-Mart Distribution Center just to shut it down."

"How do you know it didn't walk onto the asphalt by itself?" I ask.

"They had its stomach pumped and it was full of lettuce," Rich replies.

We all roll our eyes.

Steve asks his cousin Matt, who is a first-year medical student, "Have you performed an autopsy on a desert tortoise yet?"

"Not yet," Matt responds. "Just human beings."

"Can I get anyone anything?" Ruth asks, holding her granddaughter Hannah on her hip. She looks around. No response. "Just checking."

"And you wonder why people are upset," my father says, turning to me. "It's easy for you to sit here and tell us what animals we should protect while you write poems about them as a hobby—it's not your pocketbook that's hurting."

"And is yours?" I ask, fearing I have now gone as far as my father has.

I was not aware of the background music until now—Nat King Cole singing, "Have a Merry, Merry Christmas . . ."

"I don't know," Jack says, clearing his throat, pulling himself out of his chair. "Why don't you boys tell them the real story?"

John and Richard look puzzled.

"What story?" Rich asks.

"Hardpan," Jack says.

"Never mind," my father says, grinning. "Just keep that quiet."

Richard starts giggling like a little boy.

"Tell!" We beg our grandfather.

He placed his hands on the back of the lounge. "We had twenty-two crews during the war, put all the piping in the airbases at Tooele, Salt Lake, Hill, and Ogden. I never went to bed for five years—1941, 42, 43, 44, 45—just dropped dead on this lounge from exhaustion every night. We even had work in Las Vegas putting in a big water line to the north. I was away for weeks, missing Kathryn and the boys. Then one day, I was walking along the trench when I spotted what I thought was a helmet. I bent down. It moved. I realized it was a tortoise. I picked it up, its head and feet shot back into its shell. I put him in the back of my truck and brought him home for the boys. We named him 'Hardpan.'"

He looks at his sons, smiles, and walks out of the room.

"Everybody else had a dog," my father says. "German shepherds, Doberman pinschers, black Labs. We drilled a hole in his shell and tied a long cord to it and walked him around the block."

We all look at each other.

"No kidding," Rich says. "Every day we walked him."

"Hardpan?" I ask.

"You know, the desert without rain—hardpan, no give to the sand." Dad's voice is tender.

"He was reliable, old Hardpan, you have to say that about him," Rich adds.

"Until he disappeared," Jack says, returning to his chair.

———

Gopherus agassizi. Desert tortoise. Land turtle. An elder among us. Even among my family. For some of us he represents "landlocked" like the wildlands before us. Designate wilderness and development is locked out. Find a tortoise and another invisible fence is erected. The tortoise's presence compromises our own. For others, tortoise is "land-based," a sovereign on Earth, entitled to his own desert justice. He is seen as an extension of family—human and nonhuman alike—living in arid country. His presence enhances our own. The tension tortoise inspires calls for wisdom.

These animals may live beyond one hundred years. They walk for miles largely unnoticed carrying a stillness with them. Fifteen acres may be home range and they know it well. When they feel in their bodies that it is about to rain, they travel to where water pools. They wait. Clouds gather. Skies darken. It rains. They drink. It may be days, weeks, months before their beaks touch water again.

If native mythologies are true and turtles carry the

world on their backs, the carapace of the desert tortoise is designed to bear the weight. It is a landscape with its own aesthetic. Three scutes, or plates, run down the vertebrae, hexagons, with two larger scutes on top and bottom. Four plates line either side of center. The shell is bordered by twenty-four smaller ones that seem to hold the animal in place. The plastron, or bottom of the shell, has plates that fit together like a twelve-tiled floor. The desert tortoise lives inside his own creation like a philosopher who is most at home in his mind.

In winter, the desert tortoise hibernates, but not in the manner of bears. Hibernation for reptiles is "brumation," a time of dormancy where cold-blooded creatures retire, rock-still, with physiological changes occurring independent of their body temperatures. Much remains mysterious about this time of seasonal retreat, but brumation among turtles suggests it is sparked by conditions of temperature, moisture, photoperiod, and food supply. They stir in their stone-ledged dens when temperatures rise, dens they inhabit year after year, one, two, maybe five individuals together. They leave. They forage. They mate. The females lay eggs in supple sands, two dozen eggs may be dropped in a nest. Buried. Incubated. Hatched. And then the quiet plodding of another generation of desert tortoises meets the sands.

It is a genealogy of evolutionary adaptation until *Go-*

pherus agassizi suddenly begins bumping into real estate developers after having the desert to himself for millennia.

It is 1996: A lone desert tortoise stands before a bull-dozer in the Mojave.

~

My father and the Endangered Species Act. My father as an endangered species. The Marlboro Man without his cigarette is home on the range; I will list him as threatened by his own vulnerable nature. I will list him as threatened by my emotional nature. Who dares to write the recovery plan that regulates our own constructions? He will resist me. I will resist him. He is my father. I am his daughter. He holds my birth story. I will mourn his death. We face each other.

Hand over our hearts, in the American West, united states do not exist even within our own families. "Don't Tread On Me." The snake coils. The tortoise retreats. When the dust devil clears, who remains?

My father, myself, threatened species.

I recall a statement made to me by another elder, a Mormon General Authority who feared I had chosen not to have children. Call it "Ode to the Gene Pool," a manip-ulation of theology, personalized, tailorized to move me toward motherhood, another bulge in the population.

"A female bird," he wrote to me, "has no options as to

whether she will lay eggs or not. She must. God insists. Because if she does not a precious combination will be lost forever. One of your deepest concerns rests with endangered species. If a species dies out its gene pool will be lost forever and we are all the lesser because of the loss. . . . The eggs you possess over which your husband presides are precious genes. . . . You are an endangered family."

I resist. Who will follow? Must someone follow?

—⁓—

Clouds gather. It rains. The desert tortoise drinks where water has pooled.

Who holds the wisdom? My grandfather, the tortoise, calls for the story, then disappears.

Tortoise steps.

Tortoise tracks.

Tracks in time.

One can refuse to play the game.

—⁓—

Across from where I sit is a redrock ledge. We are only a stone's toss away from the city of St. George. I am hiking with my father. He has gone on ahead.

Today is the spring equinox, equal light, equal dark—a day of truce.

I have followed tortoise tracks to this place, a den. It is

cold; the air stings my face. I did not dress warmly enough. Once again, the desert deceives as wind snaps over the ridge and rides downvalley.

The tortoise is inside. I wish to speak to him, to her, to them about my family, my tribe of people who lose money and make money without recognizing their own threatened status, my tribe of people who keep tortoises, turtles, as pets and wonder why they walk away.

"Have you heard the news today?" I pull the clipping from the local paper out of my pocket, unfold it, and read aloud:

If you're a desert tortoise living in Washington County, take this advice: Start crawling your way toward the hills north of St. George, Utah.

Come March 15, any tortoise living outside a specially designated "desert tortoise reserve" could become subject to "taking"—a biological term for the death of an animal or the destruction of its habitat.

State and federal officials on Friday signed an interlocal agreement that will set aside 61,000 acres of prime tortoise habitat as a reserve that wildlife biologists believe will secure the reptile's recovery.

On the flip side, the agreement also provides permission and means by which developers and others may "take" some 1200 tortoises and develop more than 12,000 acres of tortoise habitat outside the reserve without violating the Endangered Species Act, under which the tortoise is listed as a "threatened species."

Friday's signing ends six years of battles over the slow-moving animal, whose presence around St. George has created headaches for land developers and local governments.

"We feel confident that we're going to be able to work together and have a permit that provides for the recovery and protection of the tortoise," said Bob Williams, assistant supervisor for the Fish and Wildlife Service.

Senator Bob Bennett, R-Utah, agreed. "This is clearly a very major step toward getting the endangered species issues resolved short of the trainwreck of the spotted owl."

Between 1980 and 1990, the Washington County's population increased 86% from 26,125 to 48,560. It is projected to have between 101,000 and 139,000 people by 2010.

Implementation of the Habitat Conservation Plan is scheduled to last 20 years and cost $11.5 million."

There is no movement inside the den.

"Tortoise, I have two questions for you from Neruda:

¿Quien da los nombres y los numeros al inocente innumerable?

Who assigns names and numbers to the innumerable innocent?

¿Como le digo a la tortuga que yo le gano en lentitude?

How do I tell the turtle that I am slower than he?"

The desert tortoise is still.

I suspect he hears my voice simply for what it is: human. The news and questions I deliver are returned to me and somehow dissipate in the silence.
It is enough
to breathe, here, together.

Our shadows lengthen
while the white-petaled heart of Datura
opens and closes.

We have forgotten the option of restraint.

It is no longer the survival of the fittest but the survival of compassion.

Inside the redrock ledge, the emotional endurance of the tortoise stares back at me. I blink. To take. To be taken. To die. The desert tortoise presses me on the sand, down on all fours. The shell I now find myself inhabiting is a keratinous room where my spine is attached to its ceiling. Head, hands, feet, and tail push through six doors and search for a way home.

Tortoise steps.
Land-based. Land-locked.
Land-based. Land-locked.
Learning the slow art of revolutionary patience, I listen to
my family.

A WILD ACT

The political noise in Utah is loud since September 18, 1996, when President Clinton stood on the south rim of the Grand Canyon with Vice President Al Gore and declared 1.7 million acres of slickrock in Utah the Grand Staircase–Escalante National Monument.

What rang most places as a joyful decree, a critical step in keeping land for future loving, has roused a far darker cry elsewhere.

Sixty miles north of the great chasm, residents of Kanab, Utah, heard those words and released fifty black balloons into the blue desert sky, a warning to other states that this kind of "federal dictatorship" could happen to you. Teenage girls sobbed in the halls of Kanab High School and a former county commissioner stated simply, "Our lives are now under the jurisdiction of the United Nations."

Kane County—arid, sparsely settled, not quite gorgeous enough for millionaire retreats—now mourns the loss of "nine hundred jobs" from the proposed Andalux Mine. In the local mind, 1.7 million acres of federal public lands rich in coal has been "locked up" and the county's economic future "locked out."

Utah Senator Orrin Hatch called this preemption for the commons "the mother of all land grabs." Congresswoman Enid Greene declared the president's action "unethical." And Congressman Jim Hansen heard rumors that fourteen trees had been cut down in order to secure President Clinton's perfect photo backdrop of the Grand Canyon and named the ceremony "Treegate."

My fellow Utahns who are grousing in the name of states' rights about federal control are echoing their ancestors. The broad protection of large, sweeping landscapes in America, the designation of our national parks and monuments, has most often been accomplished not by the sentiments of local politicians and adjoining communities but by the president's hand boldly signing a proclamation in the name of the people.

The Antiquities Act of 1906 up to this point has been used 103 times by chief executives. It founded Grand Canyon National Park itself, Muir Woods, Olympic National Park, Acadia National Park, as well as all the national parks in Utah (Zion, Bryce, Capital Reef, and Arches) with the exception of Canyonlands.

When President Franklin D. Roosevelt designated a national monument near Jackson Hole, Wyoming, in 1943, the locals felt betrayed. Teton County commissioners asked how the federal government could "reconcile taking away the homes of men who are now fighting to preserve their homeland." Senator Edward Robertson declared the monument "a foul, sneaking Pearl Harbor blow." The state of Wyoming filed suit against the secretary of the interior challenging the authority by which the monument was created. The state lost its case, and the monument later became Grand Teton National Park.

"Just politics," many Utahns are crying.

It has always been politics. But here is a higher result—a resistance to our energetic capacity to invade and destroy our public lands.

Conservation is part of our enactment of democracy based upon the democratic ideals expressed by James Wilson, secretary of agriculture under President Taft: ". . . the greatest good to the greatest number for the longest time." As locals tied to the exploitive susceptibility of the land we live on, we wind up thanking our federal government for saving us from ourselves. A nation's appetite for beauty transcends a state's hunger for greed.

But there is something deeper at stake here in Utah and for that matter in North America. It has to do with knitting the wild back together.

National parks are ecological islands. They are natural

refuges surrounded by a sea of human disturbance. Insularity, however, does not ensure biological health. Conservation biologist William Newmark, a curator at the Utah Museum of Natural History, has taken basic principles of island biogeography and applied them to western parks in the United States. Local extinctions occur because, even at a million acres, the size of the island may still be too small to sustain viable populations. To breed, to mix and nourish genetic pools, to forage, animals must have natural corridors to ensure safe passage from one ecosystem to the next. The integrity of a species depends on the integrity of the land.

For example, the last red fox seen in Bryce Canyon National Park was in 1961. The spotted skunk and the white-tailed jackrabbit are missing too. Zion National Park has suffered five local extinctions. Newmark documented over forty other cases of extinction around the American West. According to Newmark's research, none of these were the result of human interference. It is simply lack of land, no natural corridors to reconnect the wild, the continuous world we have lost. The larger parks such as Yellowstone and Grand Teton—a contiguous landmass—suffered the fewest losses.

The newly created Grand Staircase–Escalante National Monument rejoins Bryce National Park to Dixie National Forest and the Box-Death Hollow Wilderness Area, which then weaves Capitol Reef National Park into

Glen Canyon National Recreation Area. It is the crucial missing puzzle piece that prevents ecological fragmentation.

I find myself standing among relatives and friends in a desert of cultural fear. In the American West, we want to possess, to control, to remain sovereign against the political pull of the East. We raise clenched fists to the wind. We are still afraid of wildness: wild places, wild acts, wild thoughts. Within this, our country's wildest monument is the Kaiparowits Plateau, the most remote land in the continental United States, the last place to be mapped, the place that has the darkest nights and the deepest silence. Those who have walked this terrain know it as "a fierce and dangerous place, and it is wilderness right down to its burning core."

When President William Jefferson Clinton signed his name to Proclamation 6920—Establishment of the Grand Staircase–Escalante National Monument—he signed a bill of health for all of us, human and nonhuman alike. It swings the doors of our imagination wide open.

THE EROTIC LANDSCAPE

There is an image of a woman in the desert, her back arched as her hands lift her body up from black rocks. Naked. She spreads her legs over a boulder etched by the Ancient Ones; a line of white lightning zigzags from her mons pubis. She is perfectly in place, engaged, ecstatic, and wild. This is Judy Dater's photograph "Self-Portrait with Petroglyphs."

To be in relation to everything around us, above us, below us, earth, sky, bones, blood, flesh, is to see the world whole, even holy.

Another woman stands on her tiptoes, naked, holding draped fabric close to her body as it cascades over her breasts, down her belly and legs, like water. A strand of pearls hangs down her back; her eyes are closed.

This photograph, taken at Studio d'Ora in Vienna in

1934, is the first image I see in Det Erotiske Museum in Copenhagen, Denmark. I take another step into the foyer and find myself confronted with a six-foot golden phallus mounted on a pedestal. I am tempted to touch it, as I recall the bronze statues of women in museums around the world whose breasts and buttocks have been polished perfectly by the hands of men, but I refrain.

A visitor to this museum in Copenhagen can wander through four floors of exhibits ranging from a solitary Greek vase, circa 530 B.C., depicting Pan chasing Echo, to a wax tableau of Fanny Hill, 1749, to a prostitute's room reconstructed from an 1839 Danish police report.

Spiraling up to the fourth floor (you may choose to descend at this point to the Aphrodite Café for coffee and pastries), the visitor arrives at the Erotic Tabernacle, the climax of this museum experience. Here, you are assaulted with twelve television screens, four across and three down, which together create a montage of pornography from 1929 through 1990, complete with the music of Pink Floyd's "The Wall."

As I watch these images of men and women simultaneously moving from one position to the next, I wonder about our notion of the erotic—why it is so often aligned with the pornographic, the limited view of the voyeur watching the act of intercourse without any interest in the relationship itself.

I wonder what walls we have constructed to keep our true erotic nature tamed. And I am curious why we continue to distance ourselves from natural sources.

What are we afraid of?

The world we frequently surrender to defies our participation in nature and seduces us into believing that our only place in the wild is as spectator, onlooker. A society of individuals who only observe a landscape from behind the lens of a camera or the window of an automobile without entering in is perhaps no different from the person who obtains sexual gratification from looking at the sexual play of others.

The golden phallus I did not touch, in the end, did not touch me. It became a stump, a severance of the body I could not feel.

Eroticism, being in relation, calls the inner life into play. No longer numb, we feel the magnetic pull in our bodies toward something stronger, more vital than simply ourselves. Arousal becomes a dance with longing. We form a secret partnership with possibility.

I recall a day in the slickrock country of southern Utah where I was camped inside a small canyon outside Kanab. Before dawn, coyotes yipped, yapped, and sang. It was a chorus of young desert dogs.

The sun rose. There is a silence to creation. I stood and

faced east, stretched upward, stretched down, pressed my hands together.

I knelt on the sand still marked by the patter of rain and lit my stove, which purred like my cat at home. I boiled water for tea, slowly poured it in my earthen cup, then dipped the rose hip tea bag in and out until the water turned pink. My morning ritual was complete as I wrapped my hands around the warmth of the cup and drank.

Not far, an old juniper stood in the clearing, deeply rooted and gnarled. I had never seen such a knowledgeable tree. Perhaps it was the silver sheen of its shredded bark that reminded me of my grandmother, her windblown hair in the desert, her weathered face, the way she held me as a child. I wanted to climb into the arms of this tree.

With both hands on one of its strongest boughs, I pulled myself up and lifted my right leg over the branch so I was straddling it. Leaning back into the body of the juniper, I brought my knees up to my chest and nestled in— hidden, perfectly shaded from the heat. I had forgotten what it felt like to really be held.

Hours passed, who knows how long; the angle of light shifted. Something had passed between us, evident by the change in my own countenance, the slowing of my pulse, and the softness of my eyes as though I was awakening from a desert trance.

I finally inched my way down, wrapping my hands

around the trunk. Feet on Earth. I took out my water bottle and saturated the roots. Pink sand turned red. I left the desert in a state of wetness.

"The erotic has often been misnamed by men and used against women," says Audre Lord in *Uses of the Erotic.*

It has been made into the confused, the trivial, the psychotic, and plasticized sensation. For this reason, we have turned away from exploration and consideration of the erotic as a source of power and information, confusing it with the pornographic. But pornography is a direct denial of the power of the erotic, for it represents the suppression of true feeling. Pornography emphasizes sensation without feeling.

———

Without feeling. Perhaps these two words are the key, the only way we can begin to understand our abuse of each other and our abuse of the land. Could it be that what we fear most is our capacity to feel, and so we annihilate symbolically and physically that which is beautiful and tender, anything that dares us to consider our creative selves? The erotic world is silenced, reduced to a collection of objects we can curate and control, be it a vase, a woman, or wilderness. Our lives become a piece in the puzzle of pornography as we go through the motions of daily intercourse without any engagement of the soul.

A group of friends gather in the desert—call it a pilgrim-age—at the confluence of the Little Colorado and the Colorado Rivers in the Grand Canyon. It is high noon in June, hot, very hot. They walk upstream, men and women, moving against the current of the turquoise water. Nothing but deep joy can be imagined. Their arms fan the air as they teeter on unstable stones, white stones in the river. They are searching for mud the consistency of mousse and find it, delicious, milk chocolate mud, perfect for bathing. They take off their clothes and sink to their waists, turn, roll over, and wallow in pleasure. Their skins are slippery with clay. They rub each other's bodies; arms, shoulders, backs, torsos, even their faces are painted in mud, and they become the animals they are. Blue eyes. Green eyes. Brown eyes behind masks. In the heat, lying on ledges, they bake until they crack like terracotta. For hours, they dream the life of lizards.

In time, they submerge themselves in the Little Colorado, diving and surfacing freshly human.

D. H. Lawrence writes: "There exist two great modes of life—the religious and the sexual." Eroticism is the bridge.

The Erotic Museum in Copenhagen opened July 26, 1992. It closed August 31, 1993, because of financial difficulties. More than 100,000 visitors from around the world had paid to see erotica on display.

Standing on the sidewalk next to the red banners that advertise the museum, I watched each object, each exhibit, each wax figure, being carried out of the white building and loaded into two Volvo moving vans on Vesterbrogade 31, minutes away from Tivoli Gardens, where harlequins danced.

That was Labor Day weekend, 1993. Seven months later, the museum opened once again. The vision of Ole Ege, the founder of the Erotic Museum, is being celebrated once again, this time in a new location and with a more solid base of support.

"Denmark has been liberated sexually for twenty-five years," he says. "But we are not yet liberated in our minds. It is a matter of individual morality how one conceives this subject. For me, eroticism relates to all the highest and finest things of life. Every couple on Earth participates in this confirmation of creation, the urge we have to share ourselves, to make each other whole."

The idea that governs an erotic museum and the ideal behind an erotic life may never find a perfect resolution. Here lies our dilemma as human beings: Nothing exists in isolation. We need a context for eros, not a pedestal, not a video screen. The lightning we witness crack and charge a night sky in the desert is the same electricity we feel in ourselves whenever we dare to touch flesh, rock, body, Earth. We must take our love outdoors where reciprocity replaces voyeurism, respect replaces indulgence. We can choose to photograph a tree or we can sit in its arms, where we are participating in wild nature, even our own.

The woman in the desert stands and extends her arms.

She speaks: *"Let the beauty of what we love be what we do. There are hundreds of ways to kneel and kiss the ground."* (*Rumi*)

A LETTER TO DEB CLOW

Dearest Deb:

You asked me why I write and I said I couldn't talk about it, that it was too close, too visceral. We went on to another subject and then we finished our conversation and hung up the phone. I thought I left the question with you.

It is just after 4:00 A.M., I can't sleep. I was dreaming about Moab, Brooke and I walking around the block just before dawn. I threw a red silk scarf around my shoulders and then began reciting in my sleep why I write:

I write to make peace with the things I cannot control. I write to create red in a world that often appears black and white. I write to discover. I write to uncover. I write to meet my ghosts. I write to begin a dialogue. I write to imagine things differently and in imagining things differently perhaps the world will change. I write to honor beauty. I write to correspond with my friends. I write as a daily act of improvisation. I write because it creates my composure. I write against power and for democracy. I write myself out of my nightmares and into my dreams. I write in a solitude born out of community. I write to the questions that shatter my sleep. I write to the answers that keep me complacent. I write to remember. I write to forget. I write to the music that opens my heart. I write to quell the pain. I write to migrating birds with the hubris of language. I write as a form of translation. I write with the patience of melancholy in winter. I write because it allows me to confront that which I do not know. I write as an act of faith. I write as an act of slowness. I write to record what I love in the face of loss. I write because it makes me less fearful of death. I write as an exercise in pure joy. I write as one who walks on the surface of a frozen river beginning to melt. I write out of my anger and into my passion. I write from the stillness of night anticipating—always anticipating. I write to listen. I write out of silence. I write to soothe the voices shouting inside me, outside me, all around. I write because of the humor of our condition as humans. I write because I believe in words. I write because I do not believe in words. I write because it is a dance with paradox. I write because you can play on the page like a child left alone in the sand. I write because it belongs to the force of the moon: high tide, low tide. I write because it is the way I talk long walks. I write as a bow to wilderness. I write because I believe it can create a path in darkness. I write because as a child I spoke a different language. I write with a knife carving each word through the generosity of trees. I write as ritual. I write because I am not employable. I write out of my inconsistencies. I write because then I do not have to speak. I write with the colors of memory. I write as a witness to what I have seen. I write as a witness to what I imagine. I write by grace and grit. I write out of indigestion. I write when I am starving. I write when I am full. I write to the dead. I write out of the body. I write to put food on the table. I write on the other side of procrastination. I write for the children we never had. I write for the love of ideas. I write for the surprise of a beautiful sentence. I write with the belief of alchemists. I write knowing I will always fail. I write knowing words always fall short. I write knowing I can be killed by my own words, stabbed by syntax, crucified by both understanding and misunderstanding. I write out of ignorance. I write by accident. I write past the embarrassment of exposure. I keep writing and suddenly, I am overcome by the sheer indulgence, the madness, the meaninglessness, the ridiculousness of this list. I trust nothing, especially myself, and slide headfirst into the familiar abyss of doubt and humiliation and threaten to push the delete button on my way down, or madly erase each line, pick up the paper and rip it to shreds—and then I realize, it doesn't matter, words are always a gamble, words are splinters of cut glass. I write because it is dangerous, a bloody risk, like love, to form the words, to say the words, to touch the source, to be touched, to reveal how vulnerable we are, how transient we are. I write as though I am whispering in the ear of the one I love.

Back to sleep.
I love you,

Terry

CHANGING CONSTELLATIONS

I have never learned the constellations; my eyes have been focused too intently on Earth. But lately, my gaze has turned upward and I think I know why. The view before me, all around Little Tree Hill, has become too painful. Everywhere I look I see cuts in the landscapes, open wounds, gashes. I hear the roar and gnashing teeth of backhoes digging another hole in the ground for habitation. Wherever I walk on the streets of Salt Lake City, I am seeing changes I can no longer bear. Too many cars, too many people, too many diversions beneath a ceiling of brown smog. In winter, we call it an inversion, our inability to see the sky. We have become used to it, consider it part of our residency along the Wasatch Front. Never mind the depression that follows, that we fail to make the connection between a lack of sunlight and a lack of joy. As urban dwellers, we simply get up every morning and go to work.

I stopped working. I could not write.

Every morning I would get up earlier and earlier to grasp the silence of the canyon where we live. If I was up at 4:00 A.M. I had three hours of quiet before the chatter, shrieks, and clamoring of construction began. Before ignition, before the turn of a key, before the metal jaws of the backhoes would bite into the scrub oak and spit out their roots, I watched every tree that was being torn out of Little Tree Hill, every thicket ripped apart and tossed into a scrap pile. With each tear in the mountain's side, I felt part of my belly being ripped open.

I am aware that my own house, the home we live in and love, devoured this land. A hole was dug, a foundation was poured out of concrete, trees cut from a forest were felled, milled, and delivered, a house was constructed. My rational self understands the inevitability of growth and my own role inside it. But what I find harder and harder to abide is not growth, but the growth of greed.

The canyon where we live has suddenly become chic. It used to be the haunt of the strange, the eccentric, the Bohemian element of Salt Lake City. Now, it is becoming "suburbia in the woods," houses for the rich, ten-thousand-square-foot homes built for one or two people. In India, one street of these houses could accommodate a village in a style that would be unimaginable.

"Whine, whine, whine," my father says. "You cannot stop development, you cannot stop progress, much less run from it. It will only follow you."

This may be true, but what I have discovered for myself is that my spirit is shrinking in direct proportion to the shrinking landscape and vista. As wildness disappears, so does my peace of mind. I can no longer live here in joy.

William J. Lines, an Australian writer, notes, "The idea of progress persists only because we have forgotten more than we have remembered."

I do not want to forget Little Tree Hill with its lone, sweet mountain mahogany silhouetting the sky.

The large house going up on Little Tree Hill, which the owner has renamed after himself, henceforth called "Ross's Mountain," has made me crazy, insane, mad. My neighbors know it, sense it, try to calm my hysteria, but it doesn't help. They see me sitting on the porch naked, my arms flailing up and down in despair. Once a neighbor saw me sitting near the dry creek bed by the mailboxes, my head in my hands, and asked me if I needed a bottle of tequila. On another day, I was seen walking my cat around the block in my nightgown. The only thing that stops the pain is when I walk up Little Tree Hill, sit on its summit and feel the strength that still remains in rock, roots, and the hearty plants that will survive.

One day, a friend and I walked up to the wound, pulled the orange survey tape off the branches of scrub oak and stretched it, tore it into short strips. We pulled out the developer's stakes and, two by two, turned them into crosses, crucifixes, wrapping the orange tape tightly around the intersection of wood, and then planted them back into the dry clay soil. Just as we finished, a swarm of dragonflies descended upon us, winged crosses, translucent blue. We believed these small acts of defiance could raise the dead.

Now, I do not. They were, in fact, acts of madness, desperation. And I am not proud of what I have done. I do not believe we can stop growth any more than we can shunt our own evolution. It is our nature to expand.

What interests me is what astrophysicists are telling us about the status of the universe; in the post–big bang expansion of space, there is a recession of galaxies. When I hear the questions they are asking—"*Do we live in flat space or curved space or both?*" "*Might we actually live in a ten-dimensional universe?*"—I feel such excitement over all we do not know. Their theory of a hyperbolic universe translates in my mind to magnetic poetry, particles so small, concepts so large, like the existence of neutralinos, minuscule particles that rain down on us during the day and filter back up through us in the night, from the earth to the universe; these thoughts spark a narrative of hope in me so bright, I believe them when they say shine matters, that the way we measure the mass of a star is through its light. We can weigh the galaxy by measuring light.

But stars equal only a small amount of the total mass of the universe: 0.004 percent.

Is there some as yet undetected form of matter in the universe? Yes, astrophysicists are saying, yes, and this undetected form of matter is dark matter, a matter that does not shine. Call it the space between the stars. How do we know it is there? By measuring how fast the galaxies fall or move in a galaxy cluster we can determine mass.

Cold dark matter is named "WIMPS" by astrophysicists, meaning "weakly interacting massive particles." They are asking us to ponder neutralinos, axions, quark nuggets, elements of dark matter. Hot dark matter. Thirty percent of the mass of the universe is dark matter.

I do not begin to understand what it is they are speaking of. I am a writer in search of metaphors, and what I hear is that just as there is light in the universe—starlight —there is also darkness, a dark matter that is denser and more mysterious than anything we have yet encountered. This discovery, this knowledge, does not scare me, it allows me to pursue and stand with my own dark matter and acknowledge its weight. I believe it is our only way out of despair toward a faith in our future.

Where is the rest of matter in the universe? They tell us it is in the form of hot gas residing within groups of galaxies. I understand the power of swirling gases as the power and potency of the imagination that circles us.

I love hearing our astrophysicists talk about "the ultimate Copernican Principle": *There is nothing special about our place in the universe, even the stuff of our bodies that planets and stars are made of.*

We are insignificant. Even the stuff of our bodies, our beautiful bodies, this beautiful Earth, is not the most important stuff of the universe.

So where else can we find the mass and energy density of the universe?

Observations point to the existence of a constant vacuum energy density—70 percent.

What is this energy density due to?

We do not know.

In all our sophistication, we do not know.

What do astrophysicists tell us about the future? The universe will likely expand forever, accelerate to higher and higher speeds, becoming a colder and more lonely place to live.

This I understand.

I touch the Earth because there are so many things I do not see.

—*Alex Caldiero*

One afternoon, Brooke and I drove from Salt Lake City down to Moab, about four hours south, to meet a friend from the East for dinner. After a lovely meal and the nourishment of good conversation, we decided to simply throw down our sleeping bags on the slickrock, thirty miles from nowhere. Flat on our backs on the spine of sandstone, we were suddenly speechless, staring up at stars.

There, to the north, Polaris. We trace Capricorn to the south, Scorpio to the west. And there, looming above the purple black horizon, Jupiter. We pass the binoculars around as though we are watching birds, our glasses pointing straight up. Inside the magnification of these lenses, we watched whole galaxies, clusters of stars, even the Milky Way, which seemed to wrap us inside a gossamer shawl.

We didn't sleep all night. A shooting star here, another one there, each meteor seeming to burn a trail of memory into the night sky. My thoughts took on the density of waves, my mind so open, so pliable, each idea swelling, rising, and breaking over the other. For the first time in months, I began composing sentences.

At dawn, a red band outlined the jagged horizon that circled around us, highlighting sandstone arches and windows.

The next day, driving east alongside the Colorado River, Brooke and I turned south into a little valley at the base of Castleton Tower and the LaSal Mountains. We saw a small, simple house made of wood, stone, and glass. We walked inside, smiled, and said, "*This is the place.*"

We drove back to Salt Lake City in a daze but with hearts strong enough to risk all that was secure, to put our house up for sale, to move away from the embrace of our families.

Hands on the earth, on top of Little Tree Hill, I look up to the stars for guidance, the stars I can no longer see, stars kept from us through a conspiracy of city lights.

Am I running or am I returning to the place where my animal body resides?

The Promise of Parrots

When my great-grandmother Vilate Lee Romney died, my grandmother Lettie asked for only one thing among her few possessions, a pair of alabaster bookends carved in the shape of parrots. "From Mexico," she said. "Mother wrapped these in silk and carried them across the border from Colonia Dublan believing we would find another home."

These parrot bookends now reside on my bookshelf in the desert. I caress their smooth white bodies and think about what we choose to follow, what it means to follow, abandoning all that is safe and secure.

In 1885 the United States government was pressing down hard against plural marriage within the Deseret Territory. The president of the Mormon Church, John Taylor, moved quickly to set up "A City of Refuge" in the state of Chihuahua in Mexico for those "Latter-day Saints" in danger of being indicted (which meant conviction) on charges of polygamy. Word traveled quickly to polygamist families in Arizona and Utah and another migration ensued, one that would last for years, establishing nine colonies in Mexico.

The Romneys, my mother's kin, were among those families that fled the United States to seek both religious and political cover across the border.

My grandmother, Lettie Romney Dixon, was born in Colonia Dublan on June 12, 1909, to Vilate Lee and Park Romney. One year later she would be part of the Mormon–Mexican Exodus, where twenty-three hundred women and children were forced to leave their homes in the colonies under orders from General Salazar. Pancho Villa was leading the revolution. He wanted the Mormons "to go home."

A deal was struck between the revolutionaries and the Mormons led by President Junius Romney, Lettie's uncle, that the Mormons would be allowed to move their families to the United States without harm, after which all guns and ammunition would be turned over to the rebels.

Nights before the Saints knew they would have to abandon their homes, apple orchards, schools, and church, they danced.

From the journal of Bishop George T. Sevey:

How could this happen to them? Hadn't they been assured time and again that they were where the Lord wanted them? . . . Local Prophets from church pulpits had testified their belief that this was one of the special places of refuge for the saints when calamitous times would come upon the earth.

Nevertheless, no dancing anywhere was ever enjoyed more than those lively steps, marked by the vigorous notes of the fiddle, accompanied by the sonorous vamping of the organ. God was still in his Heaven, and all was right with the world . . .

On the morning of June 30, 1910, preparations for the Exodus had begun. . . . The decision was that all wagons would meet at the public square loaded and ready to move by sunup of the 31st of July, 1912 . . . With saddened hearts, we proceeded on our journey. . . . The men of Colonia Dublan left on August 2 by horseback.

My grandmother, a toddler of twelve months, was strapped to the back of her mother, Vilate, who was pregnant with her second child. They left town on horseback with one small saddlebag and rode to where the wagons were gathering. They had to leave so quickly, a cake was left baking in the oven.

So the story goes.

Upon arriving in El Paso, Texas, the Mormon refugees were offered a rail ticket to the town of their choice with no cost or obligation by the United States government. Once the men arrived safely, my family chose to return to

Salt Lake City, eventually settling in Cornish, Utah, where they raised sugar beets.

I know the songs that greeted them once they were back in Zion:

O ye mountains high, where the clear blue sky
Arches over the vales of the free,
Where the pure breezes blow and the clear streamlets flow,
How I've longed to your bosom to flee!
Oh, Zion, Dear Zion, land of the free,
Now my own mountain home, unto thee I have come
All my fond hopes are centered in thee.

Though the great and the wise all thy beauties despise,
To the humble and pure thou art dear;
Though the haughty may smile and the wicked revile,
Yet we love thy glad tidings to hear.
Oh, Zion, Dear Zion, home of the free,
Though thou were forced to fly to thy chambers on high,
Yet we'll share joy and sorrow with thee.

Joy and sorrow.

Romneys, Lees, Taylors, Hatches, Judds, Martineaus, Redds, Richards, and Robinsons, dozens of families, still in Utah, some still in Mexico, all carry these stories of movement and migration in their bones.

Home was wherever their prophet chose to lead them.

"If there is a place on earth nobody wants, that is the place I am hunting for," said Brigham Young, their own American Moses.

He found it in the Desert West.

Early pilgrimages from England to New York, Illinois, Iowa, across the plains to the promised land, in the name of spiritual sovereignty, is the story of my ancestors prior to their move to Mexico. My family, both my paternal and maternal lines, followed Brother Brigham to the Great Salt Lake Desert. I can hear their voices singing down the dust as they followed their beliefs toward a new world order.

As newcomers arrived, they were organized into groups and set out to colonize new towns within the Utah Territory. In the thirty years that Brigham Young oversaw Zion, from 1847 to 1877, 360 towns had been established with a population of around 140,000 settlers, the town of Moab among them. The area covered by these colonies stretched four hundred miles wide and five hundred miles long. And some of the settlements were thousands of miles from Salt Lake City: San Bernardino, California, to the west; Cordston, Canada, to the north; south to Arizona and on into Old Mexico.

What propelled these pioneers to cast off every conceivable comfort in the name of the belief of a promised land? What gave them the courage to step into a direct confrontation with death as they set out into unknown territory? What moved them into a place of prosperity where the seeds of apple trees were joyfully thrown? How did they find the stamina to work together?

My ancestors moved and settled as a result of spiritual beliefs. They gathered in the belief of an integrated life where nature, culture, religion, and civic responsibility were woven in the context of family and community.

When I look at these alabaster parrots, these chipped bookends of my great-grandmother's that she carried back to Utah from Mexico, I am reminded of what we inherit.

I have inherited a belief in community, the promise that a gathering of the spirit can both create and change culture. In the desert, change is nurtured even in stone by wind, by water, through time.

We are eroding.

We are evolving.

We are conserving the land and we are destroying it. We are living more simply and we are living more extravagantly. We are trying to live within the limits of arid country and we are living beyond the limits of available water. We live with a sense of humility and we live with a sense of entitlement. I hold these oppositions within myself.

Brooke and I awake on a winter morning before dawn to watch the sun rise over Canyonlands. Island in the Sky.

We walk on top of the snow, a hard, wind-blown crust. Piñons and junipers offer handholds as we begin our descent on icy slickrock. Once on the rim, our legs dangling in space, we watch first light slowly traverse the deeply veined canyons below.

For as far and wide as I can see, past the Henry Mountains, beyond the canyons of the Escalante, hundreds of miles west, there is not a glimpse of civilization, no evidence of an imprint, not a road, not a building, not any sign whatsoever of human habitation, only the eroding crust of Earth splayed open like a great wound.

Aware of my own breathing, I enter the calm indifference of the Colorado Plateau. My eyes soften. The landscape blurs. The sky, so much sky, seems to lift with the swell of light. The blue horizon curves down.

I listen to the hum of dawn that exists below the silence—the sound of heat being absorbed into the rocks, the whizzing of ice between columns of sandstone, expanding and contracting, the melting of snow, the yielding sand as it warms to the acceptance of water.

Brooke, nearby, carves a small piece of sandstone in his hand with another.

Because you found the trouble-shard
in a wilderness place,
the shadow centuries relax beside you
and hear you think:

Perhaps it's true
that peace conjured two people here
out of clay vessels.
                    —Paul Celan

Not far from here, a sash made of macaw feathers was found inside a dry cave. Scarlet macaw feathers tipped with yellow are wrapped around twelve ropes of twisted yucca fiber. In the center of the sash, blue macaw feathers are again wrapped around cordage creating the design of an eagle. Over two thousand macaw feathers were used to make this sash. The red- and blue-feathered streamers that appear almost like velvet fall from a waistband made from the pelt of a tassel-eared squirrel, Abert's squirrel, found in the ponderosa forests of southeastern Utah. Rawhide strips, crinkled from use, must have acted as ties that fastened the kilt or sash around the waist. When worn, it would have become animated by the knees: red and blue streamers swaying, twirling, an eagle in flight.

Archaeologists believe this to be a ceremonial garment made by the Anasazi. Contemporary Hopi kachinas wear similar sashes in their dances; only now they are woven from cloth. The macaw feathers were most likely traded from Mexico where there were connecting roads up through the Southwest. At Casas Grandes in Chihuahua, 390 miles south of Chaco Canyon in New Mexico (near the Four Corners area), archaeologists found more than five hundred macaw skeletons, many in adobe boxes that were undoubtedly breeding pens. Whether the Anasazi collected feathers from their own captive macaws brought north or simply traded for bundles of feathers is not known.

It is speculated that the Anasazi were moving through the canyon country and that the sash was carefully folded and placed temporarily inside the alcove where they had every intention of returning for it on their way back.

Archaeologists date this sash back to A.D. 1030.

It was not seen again until 1954, when it was discovered still folded in the alcove, barely covered with sand. It is now on display at the Edge of the Cedars Museum in Blanding, Utah.

Standing before the scarlet macaw sash, I am mindful of the life, the performance, of an artifact. It begs to dance as perhaps it did almost a thousand years ago under this same desert sky, empowering a body in motion on the slickrock.

When I think of movement and migration, how one finds and creates home, I think of the promise of parrots, the small gestures of faith carried by those who choose to inhabit the Desert West.

So little stays in place. When the soul does come to rest, it is usually through devotion.

RED

... *twenty years ago a child or young person was able to differentiate 360 shades of red, and today that's down to something like 30 shades, which means the subtleties are lost to the pure, heavy impact of red.*

—An Interview with Joseph Chilton Pearce,
Wild Duck Review IV: no. 2

The subtleties of our own perceptions are being lost to time. No time to enter the deep color of red. No time to contemplate how "colours appear in the neighborhood of others." There are colored shadows in the desert.

Goethe gives us the formula in his classic, *Theory of Colour:*

One of the most beautiful instances of coloured shadows may be observed during the full moon. The candle-light and moon-light may be contrived to be exactly equal in force; both shadows may be exhibited with equal strength and clearness, so that both colours balance each other perfectly. A white surface being placed opposite the full moon, and the candle being placed a little on one side at a due distance, an opaque body is held before the white plane. A double shadow will then be seen: that cast by the moon and illumined by the candle-light will be a powerful red-yellow; and contrariwise, that cast by the candle and illumined by the moon will appear of the most beautiful blue.

With a piece of white paper, a burning candle, and my back to the moon, I watched the magic of primary colors throbbing in the shadows of a feather.

There is magic in the world. Call it science. Call it religion. Call it color.

When I worked at the American Museum of Natural History in New York, I discovered the *Naturalist's Color Guide,* written by Frank B. Smithe. The text and color chips (similar to those one collects at a paint store) enthralled me, enveloped me in a world beyond the dualities of black and white. The purpose of the guide was to give ornithologists and other biologists an accurate description of the color of birds—specific plumages, a gorget of a hummingbird, the speculum on a duck's wing. It is based on the pioneering work of Robert Ridgeway, who wrote

Nomenclature of Colors . . . for Ornithologists, first published in 1886.

Other books followed. In 1912, Ridgeway published a more ambitious book entitled *Color Standards,* listing 1,115 named colors. New colors were added. Others were discarded. And in time, more sophisticated color systems were advanced, such as the Munsell Color System, specifically designed to define a color precisely with its own notations and formula. It divides a color into three parts: the spectral color, called *hue;* the degree of lightness or darkness, called *value;* and the intensity or saturation, called *chroma.*

A language of color has emerged.

Consider the range of red as described in the *Naturalist's Color Guide* with its species citations: *magenta* (a reddish color with a strong cast of purple), associate it with Lucifer hummingbird, Costa Rican wood-star, Costa's hummingbird, Heloise's hummingbird; *vinaceous, deep vinaceous* (hues ranging from purplish reds through orange and tones from pale to dark—forty-five varieties according to Ridgeway), locate the color on Verreaux's dove, Martinique dove, ruddy pigeon, pale-vented pigeon, scorched horned lark; *carmine* (described as rich crimson, bluish red, of the organic pigment produced from cochineal), see it on the red-breasted sapsucker, pileated woodpecker, ruby-and-topaz hummingbird, yellow-lored parrot, white-winged crossbill, to name just a few.

And the lists go on and on. *poppy red:* red-faced warbler, red-winged blackbird, summer tanager; *rose red:* rose-breasted grosbeak; *geranium:* quetzal; *scarlet:* cardinal; *flame scarlet:* Baltimore oriole.

What do we see in the spectrum of red?

Where I live, the open space of desire is red. The desert before me is red is rose is pink is scarlet is magenta is salmon. The colors are swimming in light as it changes constantly, with cloud cover with rain with wind with light, delectable light, delicious light. The palette of erosion is red, is running red water, red river, my own blood flowing downriver; my desire is red. This landscape can be read. A flight of birds. A flight of words. Red-winged blackbirds are flocking the river in spring. In cattails, they sing and sing; on the riverbank, they glisten.

Can we learn to speak the language of red?

The relationship between language and landscape is a marriage of sound and form, an oral geography, a sensual topography, what draws us to a place and keeps us there. Where we live is at the center of how we speak.

On the Colorado Plateau, there are speakers native to these lands: Ute, Paiute, Navajo, Hopi, Hualapai, Havasupai, and Zuni. Their vocabulary is based on kinship, shared stories, and a long history of inhabiting the desert.

When you were born and took your first breath, different colors
and different kinds of wind entered through your fingertips
and the whorl on top of your head. Within us, as we breathe,
are the light breezes that cool a summer afternoon,
within us the tumbling winds that precede rain,
within us sheets of hard-thundering rain,
within us dust-filled layers of wind that sweep in from the
                                             mountains,
within us gentle night flutters that lull us to sleep.
To see this, blow on your hand now.
Each sound we make evokes the power of these winds
and we are, at once, gentle and powerful.

—*Luci Tapahonso*
Sháá Áko Dahjiníłeh
"Remember the Things They Told Us"

Native people understand language as an articulation of kinship, all manner of relations. To the Diné, *hózhǫ* honors balance in the world, a kind of equilibrated grace, how human beings stand in relation to everything else. If a native tongue is lost, the perceived landscape is also lost. Conversely, if the landscape is destroyed, the language that evolved alongside is also destroyed.

Where am I to find my center of gravity linguistically? How do I learn to speak in a language native to where I live?

Native tongues.

Adopted tongues.

I want to learn the language of the desert, to be able to translate this landscape of red into a language of heat that quickens the heart and gives courage to silence, a silence that is heard.

I want to learn how to speak the language of red.

Red cries out for the body; open the body and it bleeds.

There is danger with red. Red is rage is hot, too hot to touch, a burn on the hand, quick to destroy. I know my own anger as lightning, its searing power capable of blistering skin. The reactionary stance of red lacks wisdom; it can hurt more than heal. To *see red* is to see destruction.

But to see red over time is to understand its capacity to transform. White horses in our valley eventually turn red.

The redrock desert of southern Utah teaches me over and over again: red endures. Let it not be my rage or anger that endures, but a passion for the bloodroot country of my burning soul that survives.

"Red is the most joyful and dreadful thing in the physical universe," G. K. Chesterton writes. "It is the fiercest note, the highest light."

Red is the first color perceived by babies and the first hue to reawaken the senses after one has been unexposed to light for an extended period of time. It is the longest wavelength and the fastest color to catch the eye, and always, red sits on top of the rainbow.

Red is the color of water in the desert.

Red: red sand, red dirt, red clay brought into our homes daily through the soles of our feet. You can't get rid of it. Where we live, red is endemic, finding its way into every opening, large or small, seeping into each pore of the skin, staining fingers and toes. We take red baths in the river, dust baths in the afternoon. At night, red dirt colors our dreams as we rub our eyes, scratch our eyes, sneeze, cough, as each red particle of sand works its way into the nucleus of every living, breathing, multiplying cell.

On a white concrete floor in a white room in Barcelona is an array of tongues, tongues made from the various soils of Spain: a conversation of ocher, yellow, white, red, black, gray, lavender, pink, brown, and beige. These earth-based tongues are extended, reclining, curled, twisted, erect, folded, waved, vertical, horizontal, bent.

Painted on the front wall are profiles of people in speech.

Painted on the back wall are the names of places where these native tongues were found: Zaragoza, Montserrat, Caceras, Rio Ebro, Cadaques, Volca del Croscat, Olot, Burgos, Figueres, Tarazona.

This is the installation of artist Jackie Brookner. She says that the first substance in her work is the soil, the raw matter of organic life. She has been traveling through

Spain collecting soils from Central Spain and Catalonia, focusing on different colors, textures, and appearances. The organic nature of speech is the confluence of earth and sound.

It is spoken and it is read.

Standing in the midst of these native tongues, I stand inside my own diction of desire and play. To stick out one's tongue. To kiss with one's tongue. To bite one's tongue. To speak with forked tongue. Tongue-tied. Tongue-twisted. Ahhhh, let me see your tongue. Open wide. I see our geographic tongues and they are red.

Can we learn to speak a language indigenous to the heart?

The colored shadows that fall from the full moon are music heard and held in the feather of a red-shafted flicker. The flicker flies. A fire burns. Love is as varied as the spectrum red. Break my heart with the desert's silence. My tongue aches and swells, touches the roof of my mouth. I begin clicking my tongue like the call blackbirds make when they fear they are alone on the river.

ODE TO SLOWNESS

Is it possible to make a living by simply watching light? Monet did. Vermeer did. I believe Vincent did too. They painted light in order to witness the dance between revelation and concealment, exposure and darkness. Perhaps this is what I desire most, to sit and watch the shifting shadows cross the cliff face of sandstone or simply to walk parallel with a path of liquid light called the Colorado River. In the canyon country of southern Utah, these acts of attention are not merely the pastimes of artists, but daily work, work that matters to the soul of the community.

This living would include becoming a caretaker of silence, a connoisseur of stillness, a listener of wind where each dialect is not only heard but understood.

Can we imagine such a livelihood?

I now live in a village in the desert. Although we have left the city, it has taken my body months to slow down, to recover a rhythm in my heart that moves my body first and my mind second. I am learning that there is no such thing as wasting time, as whole days pass inside the simple tasks of making a home, meeting new neighbors, watching the ways of deer. My ears have just now stopped ringing as they adjust, accommodate this quiet, this calm in this landscape of time.

I am reading again. Poetry. Lines seem to dangle from my hair and I wear them as adornments through the sage flats, each sentence a gift.

Whosoever has allowed the language of lovers to enter them, the language of wound and pain and solitude and hope. Whosoever has dug in the miracle of the earth. Mesmerizing dirt, earth, word.

— Carole Maso.

The poets are my companions here, alongside meadowlarks, yellow flashes of joy.

Hearing their voices now, meadowlarks calling to one another in the sage, makes me realize how lonely I had become in the city, how much I had missed their music, the conversation of birds.

The speed of my life in Salt Lake City was its own form of pathology: drive here, meet there, talk, eat, talk, listen, look at my watch, run to work, teach, more meetings, talk, listen, talk, listen, run to the health club, run some errands, shop, buy, load the car, drive the car, car in traffic, too much traffic, speed, brake, speed, brake, red light, green light, hurry home, almost home, pick up mail, pick up phone, call, talk, call, talk, time for dinner, go out for dinner, drive to dinner, eat, talk, drive, return home, bathe, read, sleep, wake, eat, dress, drive, drive to work, work, work—and the next day moved right on schedule.

If you had asked, I would have told you I was happy. My husband and I were comfortable in our urban routine, but one night over dinner, he said, "What if we are only living half-lives? What if there is something more?"

We wanted more.

We wanted less.

We wanted more time, fewer distractions. We wanted more time together, time to write, to breathe, to be more conscious with our lives. We wanted to be closer to wild places where we could walk and witness the seasonal changes, even the changing constellations. And so we banked on the idea of a simpler life away from the city near the slickrock country we love. What we would lose in income, we would gain in sanity.

We moved. Slowly, we are adjusting. We saunter more and drive less. We rarely eat out. We go to bed earlier and rise with first light. The closest town is twenty-five miles away. Friends call this a sacrifice, a lark, a momentary stay of madness. We call it home, finally.

What are we missing?

The distractions and excitement of urban life are replaced by the intensity of living in an episodic landscape where thunderstorms, flash floods, and wind break any threat of monotony. Just the other day, a dust devil carried a favorite black shawl of mine up into the air, unraveled its weave, and sent it flying toward the mesa where it was met by ravens. And at night, I am learning to see the sky as a map, the stars as thoughts, places of possibilities, kept from me by city lights.

In the vastness of the desert, I want to create my days as a ceremony around s l o w n e s s, an homage to tortoises and snakes, reptilian monks who understand what it means to move thoughtfully, deliberately, who allow the heat of sand to create currents in their blood, which massages their bones inside their leather skins.

Slowly, so slowly these creatures crawl and wind and slither across the desert measured in shadows of geologic time. This is not to say they know nothing of the wisdom of speed or hissing and hiding. They do, but in times of danger.

Speed is a response to both danger and desire.

In our human world, we worship speed and desire. We desire money. We assign money to time. What is time worth? Your time. My time. Our time. Talk fast. Work fast. Drive fast. Walk fast. Run. Who ever told us to wear jogging shoes to work? Don't saunter. Don't look. Speed walk. Speed dial. Federal Express will fly our thoughts around the world.

We do not trust slowness, silence, or stillness.

Last month, a few miles from our home, thousands of human beings were running in the desert next to the Colorado River. The river was red. It was a race; they ran shoulder to shoulder, faster and faster, bodiesbehindand-bodiesinfront, inhaling, exhaling, fat-free hearts pumping oxygen into every living cell, the body a machine, sighing, groaning, moaning like one large organism running, running, faster and faster, sweating, puking, shitting, wheezing. They outran the river, faster and faster, every one of them, two feet times thousands tapping, drumming, beating the pavement, faster and faster, running until they reached the end of the race. Stop time. Time? What was my time? What was your time? They are handed their time; for better or for worse, their trophy is their time. Where the runners stop, the river continues, a slow, strong current that now meanders through willows.

I am not so easily seduced by speed as I once was. I find I have lost the desire to move that quickly in the world. To see how much I can get done in a day does not impress me anymore. I don't think it's about getting older. It feels more like honoring the gravity in my own body in relationship to place. Survival. A rattlesnake coils, its tail shakes; the emptiness of the desert is evoked.

I want my life to be a celebration of s l o w n e s s.

Walking through the sage from our front door, I am gradually drawn into the well-worn paths of deer. They lead me to Round Mountain and the bloodred side canyons below Castle Rock. Sometimes I see them, but often I don't. Deer are quiet creatures, who, when left to their own nature, move slowly. Their large black eyes absorb all shadows, especially the flash of predators. And their ears catch each word spoken. But today, they walk ahead with their halting prance, one leg raised, then another, and allow me to follow them. I am learning how not to provoke fear and flight among deer. We move into a pink, sandy wash, their black-tipped tails look like eagle feathers. I lose sight of them as they disappear around the bend.

On top of the ridge, I can see for miles. Mesas, buttes, the sandstone folds of Fisher Towers. The light is advancing across Professor Valley as the sun begins to drop behind Porcupine Rim, creating a kaleidoscope of oranges, reds, and violets that the hand of time keeps turning minute by minute. Inside this erosional landscape where all colors eventually bleed into the river, it is hard to desire anything but time and space.

Time and space. In the desert there is space. Space is the twin sister of time. If we have open space then we have open time to breathe, to dream, to dare, to play, to pray to move freely, so freely, in a world our minds have forgotten, but our bodies remember. Time and space. This partnership is holy. In these redrock canyons, time creates space—an arch, an eye, this blue eye of sky. We remember why we love the desert; it is our tactile response to light, to silence, and to stillness.

Hand on stone—patience.

Hand on water—music.

Hand raised to the wind— Is this the birthplace of inspiration?

RIVER MUSIC

River. The river is brown is red is green is turquoise. On any given day, the river is light, liquid light, a traveling mirror in the desert.

Love this river, stay by it, learn from it. . . . It seemed to him that whoever understood this river and its secrets, would understand much more, many secrets, all secrets.
— *Siddhartha*

I love sitting by the river. A deep calm washes over me in the face of this fluid continuity where it always appears the same, yet I know each moment of the Rio Colorado is new.

"Have you learned that secret from the river; that there is no such thing as time?"

May 28, 2000—a relatively uneventful day. A few herons fly by, a few mergansers. Two rafts float through the redrock corridor. I wave. They wave back. One man is playing a harmonica, the oars resting on his lap as he coasts through flat water.

Sweet echoes continue to reach me.

I sit on the fine pink sand, still damp from high water days, and watch the river flow, the clouds shift, and the colors of the cliffs deepen from orange to red to maroon.

Present. Completely present. My eyes focus on one current in particular, a small eddy that keeps circling back on itself. Around and around, a cottonwood leaf spins; a breeze gives it a nudge, and it glides downriver, this river braided with light.

The eddy continues to coil the currents.

Boredom could catch up with me. But it never does, only the music, river music, the continual improvisation of water. Perhaps the difference between repetition and boredom lies in our willingness to believe in surprise, the subtle shifts of form that loom large in a trained and patient eye.

I think about a night of lovemaking with the man I live with, how it is that a body so known and familiar can still take my breath all the way down, then rise and fall, the river that flows through me, through him, this river, the Colorado River keeps moving, beckoning us to do the same, nothing stagnant, not today, not ever, as my mind moves as the river moves.

"To find one's own equilibrium" he tells me this morning by the river. "That is what I want to learn."

He finds rocks that stand on their own and bear the weight of others. An exercise in balance and form. Downriver, I watch him place a thin slab of sandstone on a rock pedestal, perfectly poised. He continues placing pebbles on top, testing the balance. In another sculpture, he leans two flat rocks against each other like hands about to pray.

The stillness of stones, their silence, is a rest note against the music of the river.

Our shadows on the moving water are no different than those cast by the boulders on the bank. Composition. What is the composition of the river, these boulders, these birds, our own flesh? What is the composition of a poem except a series of musical lines?

River. River music. Day and night. Shadow and light. The roar and roll of cobbles being churned by the currents is strong. This river has muscle when flexed against stone, carved stone, stones that appear as waves of rock, secret knowledge known only through engagement. I am no longer content to sit, but stand and walk, walk to the river, enter the river, surrender my body to water now red, red is the Colorado, blood of my veins.

WIND

Wind. There is a reason why the redrock country of southern Utah looks the way it does. Wind. Say the word and a small breeze blows out of your mouth. Say the word again in front of a lit match and the flame will disappear. Wind. Wind. Wind. Last night, we honestly thought our house was going to blow away.

It is humbling living here, exposed to the elements of wind, water, and heat. There is no protection in the desert. We are vulnerable. It is a landscape of extremes. I find myself mirroring them: hot, cold, wet, dry. The challenge is to live in the midst of so much beauty.

Wind is spirit made manifest and it has a thousand faces: a gentle breeze, a vicious slap, a relentless voice that can conjure demons.

The night the wind would not stop, Brooke and I lay in bed with our arms around each other. In twenty-four years of living with this man, it was the first time I ever heard him say, "I am afraid." We watched the glass windows bow and bend. Our fear was that at any moment a window would shatter and we would be murdered by a knife of the wind, our throats cut before we could scream. The doors flew open. We lashed them shut. Outside furniture became tumbleweeds and a cottontail found harbor against the corner of our house. We could hear its faint whimperings. We did not sleep.

Even in its terror, I find the wind beautiful.

It begins with a subtle stirring caused by the sunlight falling on the vapors that swaddle the earth. It is fueled by extremes—the stifling warmth of the tropics, the bitter chill of the poles. Temperature changes set the system in motion: hot air drifts upward and, as it cools, slowly descends. Knots of high and low pressure gather strength or diminish, forming invisible peaks and valleys in the gaseous soup.

Gradually the vapors begin to swirl as if trapped in a simmering cauldron. Air molecules are caught by suction and sent flying. They slide across mountain ridges and begin the steep downward descent toward the barometric lows. As the world spins, it brushes them to one side but does not slow them.

Tumbling together, the particles of air become a huge, unstoppable current. Some of them rake against the earth, tousling grasses and trees, slamming into mountains, pounding anything that stands in their way. They are a force unto them-

selves, a force that shapes the terrestrial and aquatic world.
They bring us breath and hardship. They have become the
wind.

— *Jan DeBlieu*
Wind

In this country, wind is the architect of beauty, movement in the midst of peace. This is what I seek as a writer. Art is created through the collision of ideas, forces that shape, sculpt, and define thought. There is a physicality to beauty, to any creative process. Perhaps an index to misery is when we no longer perceive beauty—that which stirs the heart—or have lost a willingness to embrace change. Does the wind harass sandstone or caress it? What stone is removed and what remains? The result of this oppositional relationship of element and form is an arch, a spire, even the magnificence of Castle Rock. And it takes time. There is a peculiar patience to both wind and rock, alongside a flashpoint of the fleeting and the eternal.

Gale.

Prevail.

The wind reminds me of endurance. The wind will always return to stir things up, keep things fresh, where nothing can be taken for granted. Life is not static, comfortable, or predictable. An Episcopal prayer reads, "Come like the wind . . . and cleanse."

LABOR

Life comes, life goes, we make life . . .
But we who live in the body see with
the body's imagination things in
outline.

—Virginia Woolf,
The Waves

I forget the first time I saw this boulder, maybe thirty years ago as an adolescent traveling through Utah's red-rock desert with my family. Or maybe it was twenty-five years ago, as a young bride making a pilgrimage to this part of the world with my new husband, not only in love with him but also with this arid landscape that ignites the imagination.

Today, I return once again to the Birthing Rock.

I return because it is a stone slate of reflection, a place where stories are told and remembered. Call it my private oracle where I hear the truth of my own heart.

Yes, the actions of life are recorded, here, now, through the hands of the Anasazi, the "ancient ones," who inhabited the Colorado Plateau from A.D. 500 to 1200. Their spirits have never left. One feels their intelligence held in the rocks, etched into the rocks. This rock stands in Kane Creek Canyon, the size of a small dwelling, exposed and vulnerable, only a few miles from the town of Moab, Utah.

There she is, as she has been for hundreds of years, the One Who Gives Birth, a woman standing with her arms outstretched, her legs wide open, with a globelike form emerging. Four sets of tiny feet march up the boulder alongside her. There are other figures nearby: a large cere-monial being wearing what appears to be an elaborate headdress and necklace. It feels male but it could be fe-male. Who knows what these Anasazi petroglyphs might mean? What is translated through stone is the power of presence, even centuries old.

Deer. Mountain sheep. Centipedes. A horned figure with a shield. More footprints. And around the corner of the boulder, two triangular figures, broad shoulders with the points down, made stable by feet. From their heads, a spine runs down the center. They are joined together through a shared shoulder line that resembles the arms of a cross. A slight tension is felt between them as each pulls the other, creating the strength of scales balanced. Next to them is another figure, unattached. A long snake with nine bends in its river body is close to making contact. All this on the slate of blue sandstone that has been varnished through time; when carved it bleeds red.

Piñon. Juniper. Saltbush. Rabbitbrush. The plant world

bears witness to the human one as they surround the Birthing Rock. They are rooted in pink sands when dry, russet when wet. It is a theater-in-the-round choreographed on Navajo sandstone, reminding us of dunes that once swirled and swayed with the wind in another geologic time.

There is much to absorb and be absorbed by in this sky-biting country. At times, it is disorienting, the Earth split open, rocks standing on their heads, entire valleys appearing as gaping wounds. This is the power and pull of erosion, the detachment and movement of particles of land by wind, water, and ice. A windstorm in the desert is as vicious as any force on Earth, creating sand smoke so thick when swirling it is easy to believe in vanishing worlds. The wind and fury subside. A calm is returned but not without a complete rearrangement of form. Sand travels. Rocks shift. The sculpting of sandstone reveals the character of windgate cliffs, sheered redrock walls polished to a sheen over time.

My husband is climbing the talus slope above me. I hear a rock fall and call to him. His voice returns as an echo.

In repetition, there is comfort and reassurance.

〜

I return my attention to the Birthing Rock, this panel of petroglyphs that binds us to a deep history of habitation in place, this portal of possibilities, a woman giving birth, a symbol of continuity, past generations now viewed by future ones.

As a woman of forty-four years, I will not bear children. My husband and I will not be parents. We have chosen to define family in another way.

I look across the sweep of slickrock stretching in all directions, the rise and fall of such arid terrain. A jackrabbit bolts down the wash. Piñon jays flock and bank behind a cluster of junipers. The tracks of coyote are everywhere.

Would you believe me when I tell you this is family, kinship with the desert, the breadth of my relations coursing through a wider community, the shock of recognition with each scarlet gilia, the smell of rain.

And this is enough for me, more than enough. I trace my genealogy back to the land. Human and wild, I can see myself whole, not isolated but integrated in time and place. Our genetic makeup is not so different from the collared lizard, the canyon wren now calling, or the great horned owl who watches from the cottonwood near the creek. Mountain lion is as mysterious a creature as any soul I know. Is not the tissue of family always a movement between harmony and distance?

Perhaps this is what dwells in the heart of our nation—choice—to choose creation of a different sort, the freedom to choose what we want our lives to be, the freedom to choose what heart line to follow.

My husband and I live in this redrock desert, this "land

of little rain" that Mary Austin described at the beginning
of the twentieth century. It is still a dry pocket on the
planet one hundred years later. Not much has changed regarding the aridity and austerity of the region.

What has changed is the number of needs and desires
that we ask the earth to support. There are places where the
desert feels trampled, native vegetation scraped and cut at
their roots by the blades of bulldozers, aquifers of water re-
ceding before the tide of luxury resorts and homes.

And the weight of our species will only continue to tip
the scales.

The wide-open vistas that sustain our souls, the depth
of silence that pushes us toward sanity, return us to a kind
of equilibrium. We stand steady on Earth. The external
space I see is the internal space I feel.

But I know this is the exception, even an illusion, in
the American West, as I stand in Kane Creek where my
eyes can follow the flight of a raven until the horizon
curves down. These remnants of the wild, biologically
intact, are precious few. We are losing ground. No matter
how much we choose to preserve the pristine through our
passion, photography, or politics, we cannot forget the simple truth: There are too many of us.

Let me tease another word from the heart of a nation:
sacrifice. Not to bear children may be its own form of
sacrifice. How do I explain my love of children, yet our
decision not to give birth to a child? Perhaps it is about

sharing. I recall watching my niece, Diane, nine years old, on her stomach, eye to eye with a lizard; neither moved while contemplating the other. In the sweetness of that moment, I felt the curvature of my heart become the curvature of Earth, the circle of family complete. Diane bears the name of my mother and wears my DNA as closely as my daughter would.

Must the act of birth be seen only as a replacement for ourselves? Can we not also conceive of birth as an act of the imagination, giving body to a new way of seeing? Do children need to be our own to be loved as our own?

Perhaps it is time to give birth to a new idea, many new ideas.

Perhaps it is time to give birth to new institutions, to overhaul our religious, political, legal, and educational systems that are no longer working for us.

Perhaps it is time to adopt a much needed code of ethics, one that will exchange the sacred rights of humans for the rights of all beings on the planet.

We can begin to live differently.

We have choices before us, conscious choices, choices of conscience and consequence, not in the name of political correctness, but ecological responsibility and opportunity.

We can give birth to creation.

To labor in the name of social change. To bear down

and push against the constraints of our own self-imposed structures. To sacrifice in the name of an ecological imperative. To be broken open to a new way of being.

~

It begins to rain softly in the desert; the sand is yielding, the road is shining, and I know downriver a flash flood is likely, creating another landscape through erosion, newly shaped, formed, and sculpted.

I wonder when this catastrophic force will reach me?

Erosion. Perhaps this is what we need, an erosion of all we have held secure. A rupture of all we believed sacred, sacrosanct. A psychic scouring of our extended ideals such as individual property rights in the name of economic gain at the expense of ecological health.

I wonder when . . .

The wall of water hits. Waves turn me upside down and sideways as I am carried downriver, tumbling in the current, dizzy in the current, dark underwater, holding my breath, holding my breath. I cannot see but believe I will surface, believe I will surface, holding my breath. The muscle of the river is pushing me down, deeper and deeper, darker and darker. I cannot breathe, I am dying under the pressure, the pressure creates change, a change of heart. The river changes its heart and pushes me upward with the force of a geyser. I surface, I breathe. I am back in the current, moving with the current, floating in the current, face up, on my back. There are others around me, our silt-covered bodies navigating downriver, feet pointing downriver. We are part of the river, in boats of our own skin, finally, now our skin shining, our nerve returning, our will is burning. We are on fire, even in water, after tumbling and mumbling inside a society where wealth determines if we are heard, what options we have, what power we hold.

How can I get my bearings inside this river?

Erosion. I look up. Canyon walls crack and break from the mother rock, slide into the river, now red with the desert. I am red with the desert. My body churns in the current, and I pray the log jam ahead will not reduce me to another piece of driftwood caught in the dam of accumulation.

Who has the strength to see this wave of destruction as a wave of renewal?

I find myself swimming toward an eddy in the river, slower water, warmer water. We are whirling, twirling in a community of currents. I reach for a willow secure on the shore; it stops me from spinning. My eyes steady. The land is steady. In the pause of this moment, I pull myself out. Collapse. Rise.

Now on shore like a freshly born human, upright, I brush my body dry, and turn to see that I am once again standing in front of the Birthing Rock, my Rock of Instruction, that I have sought through my life, defied in my life, even against the will of my own biology.

No, I have never created a child, but I have created a life. I see now, we can give birth to ourselves, not an indulgence but another form of survival.

We can navigate ourselves out of the current.

We can pull ourselves out of the river.

We can witness the power of erosion as a re-creation of the world we live in and stand upright in the truth of our own decisions.

We can begin to live differently.

We can give birth to deep change, creating a commitment of compassion toward all living things. Our human-centered point of view can evolve into an Earth-centered one.

Is this too much to dream? Who imposes restraint on our imagination?

I look at the rock again, walk around to its other side, the side that is hidden from the road I experienced as a river. The panel has been shot away, nicked by bullets, scraped and chipped to oblivion.

Six small figures have survived the shooting rampage. I bend down and look more closely at the deliberate nature of these petroglyphs.

Someone cared enough to create life on a rock face, to animate an inanimate object. Someone believed she had the power to communicate a larger vision to those who would read these marks on stone, a vision that would endure through time.

I see a spiral and what appears to be a figure dancing, her arms raised, her back arched, her head held high.

We can dance; even in this erosional landscape, we can dance.

I have come full circle around the boulder.

There she is, the One Who Gives Birth. Something can pass through stone. I place one hand on her belly and the other on mine. Desert Mothers, all of us, pregnant with possibilities, in the service of life, domestic and wild; it is our freedom to choose how we wish to live, labor, and sacrifice in the name of love.

POLICE REPORT

While reading the local newspaper, the *Moab Times Independent,* I came across this tidbit in the police report (December 9, 1998):

> *An officer was dispatched on a "strange lights in the sky" call. The officer met with the RP (reporting person), who showed the lights to the officer. The officer noted that it looked somewhat like a planet, except it was changing colors; blue, green, red, yellow, etc. The officer noted that the light was way out of his jurisdiction and took no further action.*

What is within our jurisdiction and what is not?

What do we choose to act on and what do we chose to ignore?

Mary Austin's Ghost

Mary Austin haunts me. I am intimidated by her. She is a presence in my life even though she has been dead over sixty years. A photograph of her taken by Ansel Adams in 1929 sits on my desk. Austin thought the photograph was unflattering. In a letter to Adams (who hoped she would "be utterly pleased with the prints") she wrote, "I dare say you can take away that dreadful smirk, and the drawn look about the mouth . . . the carriage of the head, with the face thrust down and forward, and the slumped shoulders are not only not characteristic of me, but contradict the effect it is still necessary for me to make on my public."

This image of Mary Austin makes me smile. She was tough, cantankerous, and hardly gracious. She was difficult. Stories still circulate about her intensity, her remarkable energy, her insistence on privacy, how she would turn

on her garden hose and spray unannounced or unwel-
comed visitors to her home in New Mexico. I love that
Mary Austin was not polite or coy or particularly accom-
modating. Too many women have been silenced in the
name of "niceness." Candid and direct, she was utterly focused on her vision, and her vision was focused on the arid
lands of the West.

I view her as a sister, soulmate, and a literary mentor, a
woman who inspires us toward direct engagement with
the land in life as well as on the page. She was unafraid of
political action embracing the rights of Indian people,
women, and wildlands. Mary Austin was a poet, a pioneer,
and a patriot.

Esther Lanigan Stineman writes in *Mary Austin — Song
of a Maverick,*

> *While many Americans turned to old cathedrals and tradi-
> tions of Europe, or even to the Far East, to alleviate anxieties
> emanating from an increasingly mechanized and technolo-
> gized world, Austin found a solution in America itself.*

Mary Austin believed in wild America, in all that was
indigenous. And nowhere is this philosophy more evident
than in *The Land of Little Rain.* It was written in 1903. One
hundred years later, *The Land of Little Rain* has never been
more relevant.

Think about the California desert that Mary Austin

knew at the turn of the century and think about what it looks like today. Could she have imagined the sprawling population of Los Angeles and its unquenchable thirst that has drained her beloved Owens Valley? Consider the solitude she encountered in the Sierras and the heavy foot traffic one encounters now on the trails. And what would she say to all the off-road vehicles that have pummeled the Mojave, shattering the eardrums of kangaroo rats burrowing below the sands?

Austin writes in the opening chapter, "The Land of Little Rain," "... there is the divinest, cleanest air to be breathed anywhere in God's world. Some day the world will understand that."

Will we?

On October 31, 1994, the California Desert Protection Act passed in the Congress of the United States. After decades of opposition, 7.5 million desert acres were protected from further development. Two national parks were created, Death Valley and Joshua Tree, with the establishment of the Mojave National Preserve. In addition, 3.5 million acres were set aside as wilderness.

Then in 1995, California Congressman Jerry Lewis, a longtime antagonist of desert protection, proposed in the House of Representatives that one dollar be allocated as part of the 1996 Department of Interior appropriations bill for the Mojave National Preserve. His proposal failed thanks to a national outcry.

Finally, a year later in April, after repeated delays and the Republican drive to undermine the Desert Protection Act with riders attached to defund the Mojave, President Clinton signed the 1996 Omnibus Budget Bill, exercising his waiver rights, thereby funding the preserve.

When Mary Austin writes in "The Pocket Hunter" about a certain breed of miners who flocked to California for material wealth held in the land—"These men go harmlessly mad in time, believing themselves just behind the wall of fortune"—she could be talking about the forces behind the contemporary wise use movement and its war against the public lands in the American West.

The testimony to Austin's brilliance as a writer is in the timelessness of her prose. "This is the nature of that country," she writes. "There are hills, rounded, blunt, burned, squeezed up out of chaos, chrome and vermilion painted, aspiring to the snowline. . . ." A reader feels the depth and sensuality of her affections. "A land of lost rivers, with little in it to love; yet a land that once visited must be come back to inevitably. If it were not so there would be little told of it."

Mary Austin tells us a great deal about the beauties, frailties, and strengths of the desert, ranging from the quality of light to the practice of coyotes and buzzards to the course of waterways; "The origin of mountain streams is like the origin of tears—potent to the understanding but mysterious to the sense." She is rarely sentimental, providing a lyricism to her narrative that allows the reader not only to see the desert but to feel it in the balance of both its magnificence and its terror.

Death by starvation is slow. The heavy-headed, rack-boned cattle totter in the fruitless trails. . . . There is fear in their eyes when they are first stricken, but afterward only intolerable weariness. . . . It needs a nice discrimination to say which of the basket-ribbed cattle is likeliest to afford the next meal, but the scavengers make few mistakes. One stoops to the quarry and the flock follows.

The novelist Milan Kundera talks about "a writer's vocabulary" in *The Art of the Novel* and encourages one to create a "personal dictionary." "Put down your key words," he says, "your problem words, the words you love. . . ." Through this exercise, he maintains, a writer can begin to understand his or her themes, obsessions, and vulnerabilities. If Mary Austin were to humor him with this practice, she would undoubtedly list the word *white* among them. It appears dozens of times in *The Land of Little Rain,* with myriad meanings and imagery.

White as in the burning light of the desert, "the *white* truce of noon." White as reflective water. "By the end of the dry season the water trails of the Ceriso are worn to a *white* ribbon in the leaning grass. . . ." White as a blank spot on a map. ". . . all the paths that wild creatures use going down to the Lone Tree Spring are mapped out *whitely* from this level, which is also the level of hawks." White as the absence of color, "distinguished by the *white* patches under the wings." White as the color of dominance. "He had come into the keeping of the Paiutes as a hostage for the long peace which the authority of the *whites* made interminable. . . ." White as illumination. "The best time to visit Shoshone Land is when the deer-star hangs low and *white* like a torch over the morning hills." And white as the color of the creative spirit. "And what flower did you wear, Seyavi?" "I, ah,—the *white* flower of twining (clematis), on my body and my hair, and so I sang—."

Mary Austin's obsession with "white" convinces me of the authenticity of Mary Austin's voice. Only a well-seasoned desert wanderer knows the spell of white in arid country. It is the mirage. It is the sculpture of bleached bones. It is parched skin and a dry mouth. It is the dream of water and the wish of being home when you know you have traveled too far from comfort. White is the soul heat of *this land of little rain* that lures you deeper into the desert and invites you to lose your mind. Austin spent both real and mythic time squinting in the sun like Coyote.

For all of Austin's friends and critics who found her personally arrogant, erratic, and too bold in her behavior, an abiding and enduring compassion and humility comes through the rigors of a disciplined eye toward nature. She knew what it meant to sit still. Her prose bears patience in her impatience with us as a species: "It takes man to leave unsightly scars on the face of the earth." Her last paragraph in *The Land of Little Rain* could only have been written through the hard-earned observations of a native, an individual who understood how wildness "uncramps our souls."

Come away, you who are obsessed with your own importance in the scheme of things, and have got nothing you did not sweat for, come away by the brown valleys and full-bosomed hills to the even-breathing days, to the kindliness, earthiness....

In 1991, I was asked to read *The Land of Little Rain* as a "book on tape." Little did I know how difficult it would be to translate her language orally. Here was a cadence completely foreign to me, a narrative more ornate and elaborate than the bare-boned prose familiar to our time. I kept stumbling over words and sentences, losing my breath, then catching it, having to go back again and again to get it right and not fall into a false rhythm that made it sound forced, comical, or melodramatic. And still, I was missing her voice completely. It was only in hearing the text outloud that I realized the era that held Mary Austin. It was

Victorian diction written through the perceptions of a radical spirit. Mary Austin wrote through the lace of her age.

After hours of tedious recording, with starts and stops, retakes and edits, something happened while I was reading "The Basket Maker." For the first time, almost midsentence, I heard Mary Austin's voice. I literally *heard* her voice. It was as though she seeped into my soul, took hold of my vocal cords, and rearranged them. The quality of my voice changed. I saw Seyavi, the Paiute woman, and more importantly felt her, felt Austin's deep regard for indigenous ways and recognized this chapter not only as a descriptive essay on a woman basket maker, but also as an essay on women and their creative spirits. "Every Indian woman is an artist,—sees, feels, creates, but does not philosophize about her processes." It was Austin's empathy, even sorrow, that seized me. Between the lines I read of her own struggles with the creative process, the tension between a domestic life and an artistic one, the invisible strands that bind us together as women, fellow weavers, that transcend culture. We are all anonymous in our pain to create. The integrity of Seyavi's life that Austin so magnificently describes perhaps gave her courage, even a map, to chart this tender terrain.

The rest of the reading went quickly.

That night, I could not sleep.

Mary Austin was a mystic. She believed in the ineffable that "naked space" nourished, "exciting in the heart that subtle sense of relationship to the earth horizon which is the nurture of the spiritual life." Scholars have speculated why *The Land of Little Rain* has endured. Could it be that Austin loved the desert so much her final rebellion even in death was her refusal to leave?

The spirit of Mary Austin is still with us.

WILDERNESS AND
INTELLECTUAL HUMILITY:
ALDO LEOPOLD

I can remember exactly where and when I read *A Sand County Almanac* for the first time: Dinosaur National Monument, June 1974. My mother and grandmother were talking comfortably in their lawn chairs, my brothers were playing on the banks of the Green River, and I was sitting beneath the shade of a generous cottonwood tree.

Aldo Leopold spoke to me.

With a yellow marker in hand, I underlined the words:

Wilderness is the raw material out of which man has hammered the artifact called civilization. . . . The rich diversity of the world's cultures reflects a corresponding diversity in the wilds that gave them birth. . . .

And a few pages later: *"The ability to see the cultural value of wilderness boils down, in the last analysis, to a question of intellectual humility."*

I closed the book having finished the last two chapters, "Wilderness" and "The Land Ethic." I wanted desperately to talk to someone about these ideas, but I kept quiet and tucked Leopold into my small denim pack, not realizing what the personal impact of that paperback copy with a flaming orange sunset over wetlands would be.

I was eighteen years old.

Almost twenty-five years later, I can honestly say it is Aldo Leopold's voice I continue to hear whenever I put pen to paper in the name of wildness.

The essays of *A Sand County Almanac* were published in 1949. They were revolutionary then and they are revolutionary now. Leopold's words have helped to create the spine of the American wilderness movement.

The vision of Aldo Leopold manifested itself on the land in 1924, when he convinced the National Forest Service to designate twelve hundred square miles within the Gila National Forest as a wilderness area forty years before the Wilderness Act of 1964 was signed into law.

Aldo Leopold perceived the value of wilderness to society long before it was part of the public discourse. He has inspired us to see that in the richness of biological systems all heartbeats are held as one unified pulse in a diversified world. He understood this as a scientist and land manager, and he understood it as a natural philosopher.

When Leopold writes about "*the community concept*" and states, "*All ethics so far evolved rest upon a single premise:*

*that the individual is a member of a community of interde-
pendent parts,"* he instinctively elevates the discussion above
what one typically hears in wilderness debates—that the
land is meant for our use at our discretion, that profit dic-
tates public lands policy.

And when he takes this notion of interdependent parts
one step further and proposes that we *"[enlarge] the boundaries of community to include soils, waters, plants, and animals,
or collectively: the land,"* he challenges us. In a politically
conservative and theocratic state like Utah, this kind of
thinking can be grounds for heresy, evidence of paganism,
the preemptive strike before black helicopters fueled by
the United Nations move in to defend public lands from
the people who live there.

But what I love most about Aldo Leopold is that he
keeps moving through his lines of natural logic with an
eloquent rigor and persistence. Finally, he ruptures our
complacency and asks simply, *"Do we not already sing our
love for and obligation to the land of the free and home of the
brave? Yes, but just what and whom do we love?"*

Wilderness.

In the American West, there may not be a more explo-
sive, divisive, and threatening word.

Wilderness.

The place of a mind where slickrock canyons hold a
state of grace for eons whether or not human beings make
an appearance.

Wilderness.

The mind of a place where perfection is found through the evolutionary path of a mountain lion slinking down the remote ridges of the Kaiparowitz Plateau like melted butter.

Roadless.

   Ruthless.

      Wilderness.

"A resource which can shrink but not grow." Shrink but not grow. Aldo Leopold's words echo throughout the wildlands of North America.

Why is this so difficult for us to understand? Why as we enter the twenty-first century do we continue to find the notion of wilderness so controversial?

Perhaps Leopold would say wilderness is becoming more difficult to understand because there is less and less wilderness to be found.

Wilderness is threatening as a word because it is now threatened as a place.

How can we begin to understand what wilderness is if we have never experienced a place that is unaltered and unagitated by our own species? How are we to believe in the perfect mind of the natural world if we have not seen it, touched it, felt it, or found our own sense of proportion in the presence of wildness. If there is a greatness to the American spirit, a spirit aligned with freedom and faith, surely its origin is to be found in the expanse of landscapes that have nurtured us: coastlines, woodlands, wetlands, prairies, mountains, and deserts.

"*Shall we now exterminate this thing that made us American?*" writes Leopold. The extinction of places we love may not come as a result of global warming or a meteorite heading in our direction, but as a result of our lack of imagination. We have forgotten what wildness means, that it exists, here, now. If we continue to cut, whittle, and wager it away, stone by stone, tree by tree, we will have turned our backs on bears, wolves, cougars, mountain goats and mountain sheep, martens, fishers, wolverines, caribou, musk oxen, otters, sea lions, manatees, alligators, gila monsters, blue-collared lizards, roadrunners, song sparrows, milkweeds and monarchs, spring peepers and fireflies and the myriad other creatures with whom we share this continent.

When Leopold speaks of silphium, sedge, leatherleaf, tamarack, buffalo, bluebirds, cranes, geese, deer, and wolves, he recognizes them as family. His language of landscape evokes an intimacy born of experience. And his experience in nature, on the land, allowed him to test his ideas, to change and grow, to alter his opinions, and to form new ones. We are the beneficiaries of his own philosophical evolution.

In 1926, Aldo Leopold wrote in "A Plea for Wilderness Hunting Grounds,"

There are some of us who challenge the prevalent assumption that Christian civility is to be measured wholly by the roar of industry, and the assumption that the destruction of the wild places is the objective of civilization, rather than merely a means providing it with a livelihood. Our remnants of wilderness will yield bigger values to the nation's character and health than they will to its pocketbook, and to destroy them will be to admit that the latter are the only values that interest us.

Brave words to an America that was on the verge of the dust bowl, the Depression, and the postwar buildup. Leopold held the long view in a country spoiled by its abundance of natural resources and whose native gifts were viewed as infinite. He took his stand in the wilderness.

We continue to learn from Leopold that wilderness is not simply an idea, an abstraction, a cultural construct devised to mirror our own broken nature. It is home to all that is wild, *"blank places on a map"* that illustrate human restraint.

There are those within the academy who have recently criticized "the wilderness idea" as a holdover from our colonial past, a remnant of Calvinist tradition that separates human beings from the natural world and ignores concerns of indigenous people. They suggest that wilderness advocates are deceiving themselves, that they are merely holding on to a piece of America's past, that they are devoted to an illusory and "static past," that they are apt to "adopt too high a standard for what counts as 'natural.' " These scholars see themselves as ones who "have inherited the wilderness idea" and are responding as "Euro-American men" within a "cultural legacy . . . patriarchal Western civilization in its current postcolonial, globally hegemonic form."

I hardly know what that means.

If wilderness is a "human construct," how do we take it out of the abstract, and into the real? How do we begin to extend our notion of community to include all life-forms so that these political boundaries will no longer be necessary? How can that which nurtures evolution, synonymous with adaptation and change, be considered static? Whom do we trust in matters of compassion and reverence for life?

I believe that considerations of wilderness as an idea and wilderness as a place must begin with conscience.

I come back to Leopold's notion of "*intellectual humility.*" We are not alone on this planet, even though our behavior at times suggests otherwise. Our minds are meaningless in the face of one perfect avalanche or flash flood or forest fire. Our desires are put to rest when we surrender to a grizzly bear, a rattlesnake, or goshawk defending its nest. To step aside is an act of submission, to turn back an act of admission, that other beings can and will take precedence when we meet them on their own wild terms. The manic pace of our modern lives can be brought into balance by simply giving in to the silence of the desert, the pounding of a Pacific surf, the darkness and brilliance of a night sky far away from a city.

Wilderness is a place of humility.

Humility is a place of wilderness.

Aldo Leopold understood these things. He stepped aside for other wild hearts beating in the Gila National Forest, in the Boundary Waters, in the wetlands of the sand counties, and in the fields of his own home, where he must have puffed his pipe in admiration as the sandhill cranes circled over him at the Shack.

When contemplating Aldo Leopold and wilderness, I believe we need both intellectual humility and political courage in the days ahead. We need humility to say we may not know enough to intrude on these wildlands with our desire for more timber, more coal, more housing and development. We may have to bow our heads and admit our intellectual ceiling may be too low to accommodate the vast expanse above and inside the Grand Canyon. We will need political courage to say we need to honor and protect all the wilderness that is left on this continent to balance all the wilderness we have destroyed; we need wilderness for the health of our communities and for the health of the communities we acknowledge to exist beyond our own species. We will need both intellectual humility and political courage to say, for example, we made a mistake when we dammed Hetch Hetchy and Glen Canyon; let us take down with humility what we once built with pride. Politi-

cal courage means caring enough to explain what is perceived at the time as madness and staying with an idea
long enough, being rooted in a place deep enough, and
telling the story widely enough to those who will listen,
until it is recognized as wisdom—wisdom reflected back
to society through the rejuvenation and well-being of the
next generation who can still find wild country to walk in.

This is wilderness—the tenacious grip of beauty.

In 1974, as a self-absorbed teenager, I was unaware of
the efforts made twenty years earlier on my behalf by
people like Howard Zahniser, Margaret and Olaus Murie,
David Brower, and Wallace Stegner to keep the Green
River free-flowing through Split Mountain in Dinosaur
National Monument. Nor did I realize as I sat on its banks
that summer day that it had ever been threatened by the
Bureau of Reclamation's efforts to dam Dinosaur as part of
the Colorado River Basin Storage Project. It was a history
no one told us in Utah's public schools. All I knew was that
I felt safe enough here to continue dreaming about wildness. Aldo Leopold was tutoring me sentence by sentence
in how ecological principles are intrinsically woven into an
ethical framework of being.

Historians have said the defeat of the dam on the
Green River in Dinosaur National Monument marked the
coming of age of the conservation movement. Conserva-
tionists of my generation were born under this covenant.
The preservation and protection of wilderness became

part of our sacred responsibility, a responsibility that each generation will carry.

In order to protect that which is original in the land and in ourselves, we can draw on the intellectual humility, the political courage, the wisdom and strength of character of Aldo Leopold. His lifelong stance toward wilderness inspires us not to compromise out of expediency and social pressure in considering lifestyles over life zones. Rather, as Leopold states in *The River of the Mother of God,*

In this headlong stampede for speed and ciphers we are crushing the last remnants of something that ought to be preserved for the spiritual and physical welfare of future Americans, even at the cost of acquiring a few less millions of wealth or population in the long run. Something that has helped build the race for such innumerable centuries that we may logically suppose it will help preserve it in the centuries to come.

A Prayer for
a Wild Millennium

Our reactions to wild land are dignified and deserving . . . the long prayer in a steepled church in that time of pain and confusion.

—Charles Wilkinson,
The Eagle Bird

On New Year's Day, I went walking in Mary Jane Canyon, a few miles east of where we live, part of the Utah Wilderness Coalition's new 9.1-million-acre wilderness proposal. Inside this canyon that has eroded into the white rim sandstone, I was reminded of what endures and what is whittled and washed away by wind and water, how dynamic this landscape is where rocks tell time differently.

Castle Rock. The Priest and Nuns. Adobe Mesa. Porcupine Rim. These redrock formations have witnessed endless millennia and will survive many, many more. I watched the light shift and tarry on the windgate, painting the various sandstone layers pink, salmon, lavender, blue, bloodred, deep maroon. The creases on the rock face softened and then intensified until I began to see the character lines of topography as my own aging skin.

These wildlands matter. Call them places of Original Mind where an authentic sensibility can evolve. Wild country offers us perspective and gravity, even in an erosional landscape like the Colorado Plateau.

I have watched rockslides, waterfalls, flash floods, and dust devils take these wildlands in hand and transpose them into something new. Clear water flows red, turns muddy, then pulls the sandy bank into the river. The Colorado River is raging, scouring, sculpting the landscape. The landscape is changing. We are changing. What are we to make of our own short stay on this beloved blue planet of ours as it rotates and revolves in space?

To keep myself steady, I walk, one foot in front of the other. Small things are noticed, evidence that I am not alone: the abundance of silver berries on juniper, the grasses where deer have bedded down, the sand tracks of beetles, the dropped feather of a raven. To move through wild country in the desert or in the woods is to engage in a walking meditation, a clearing of the mind, where we remember what we have so easily lost.

Time.

Time and space.

The shape of time and space is different in wilderness. Time is something encountered through the senses not imposed upon the mind. We walk, we sit, we eat, we sleep, we look, we smell, we touch, we hear, we taste our own feral nature. What we know in a wild place is largely translated through the body.

When we are in our urban skin, what we know is largely translated through television, radio, billboards, newspapers, magazines, and the Internet, the fast-paced conversations we catch on the run. We maneuver our way through a maze of shimmering surfaces, concrete, glass, and asphalt. Speed is our adaptation to an abstract life.

In wildness, we can saunter, every step creates a more informed muscle. The depth of a canyon as it twists and turns corresponds with the surprises and complexities of our own minds now free to wander. We cover more ground than we ever thought possible. We stop at a pool and see the reflection of our post-Paleolithic selves.

In the crisp possibility of the first day of the new century, I sat on the edge of a cliff with my feet dangling, the creek bed hundreds of feet below. Looking out toward the layered pastel horizon of mesas, buttes, and the buttresses, the eerie fins of Fisher Towers looked like the draped wings of a great theater pulled back during a performance. It began to snow. I watched the blue light of winter fall across the valley. Part of me wanted to leap, not out of despair, but joy. It is a difficult impulse to explain, but I believe it has something to do with feeling very, very small and very, very large, at once.

There are those citizens who say we have enough wilderness in this country; in fact, they say we have too much. Many of my neighbors in Grand County, Utah, share this point of view. And there are others among us who believe wilderness is simply a social construct, "a received idea," an artifact in Puritan thinking that belongs to the realm of nostalgia. But there are others of us who believe we need more wilderness not less, that wilderness is not just an idea but a place, not merely an abstraction but the difference between an intact ecosystem and a fragmented one.

I believe we need wilderness in order to be more complete human beings, to not be fearful of the animals that we are, an animal who bows to the incomparable power of natural forces when standing on the north rim of the Grand Canyon, an animal who understands a sense of humility when watching a grizzly overturn a stump with its front paw to forage for grubs in the lodgepole pines of the northern Rockies, an animal who weeps over the sheer beauty of migrating cranes above the Bosque del Apache in November, an animal who is not afraid to cry with delight in the middle of a midnight swim in a phosphorescent tide, an animal who has not forgotten what it means to pray before the unfurled blossom of the sacred datura, remembering the source of all true visions.

As we step over the threshold of the twenty-first century, let us acknowledge that the preservation of wilderness is not so much a political process as a spiritual one, that the language of law and science used so successfully to define and defend what wilderness has been in the past century must now be fully joined with the language of the heart to illuminate what these lands mean to the future. Let us dare to say to those in positions of power, to our neighbors and families, to our churches and communities, that we recognize an indomitable spirit in the land and in our bones that cradles life's DNA; wilderness is the great map to our own evolution. And may we make vows as a nation in transition, to value open spaces over the value of economic sprawl.

Wildness is a deeply American value.

In the decade to come, we have bills pending to designate national parks, national forests, wildlife refuges, and wilderness areas in every western state. These bills will not translate to the preservation of what we love if we do not engage ourselves fully in social change.

We have never needed wilderness more.

Somewhere in Mary Jane Canyon, there are handprints on stone, where a small clan dipped their palms in paint—paint made from the secret pigments of place—and left their imprint of humanity on the wall.

We, too, can humbly raise our hands with those who have gone before and those who will follow. Hand on rock. We remember what we have forgotten, what we can reclaim in wildness.

ENTRY

Redstone. Heartstone. Bloodred in the company of green. See how much passionate life stands out even in this endless expanse of desert. A redstone in the sand. Simply that. It brought my body down, inspired my hand to hold one small stone. I believe in the fire of an idea.

—Journal entry,
September 8, 2000

STRIKE MOMENT

Chema Madoz is a Spanish artist who has used the simple matchstick as his *ars poetica.* He calls his installation
"Mixtos," or matches.

I absorb his images:

*A spent match is resting horizontally against the back-
ground of wood where a knot in the grain resembles a flame.
The match reignites.*

*Another burnt match is turned on its head against the num-
bered gauge of a thermometer becoming the dark mercury that
tells us the temperature is twenty-five degrees centigrade.*

*A half circle of matchsticks splayed against a horizon be-
comes the rising sun.*

A full circle of matchsticks is the full sun.

*Matches burned and curled with their heads facing diago-
nally take on the urgency of swimming sperm.*

A book of matches is opened and placed at the end of a paintbrush.

The lead of a pencil is replaced with the head of a match.

What is it that ignites an artist's soul, a writer's hand. What is responsible for that *strike moment,* when the match and band of sandpaper unite in a friction that produces flame. The strike moment of the artist creates the moment of illumination for the viewer.

Democracy is full of strike moments, when injustice rubs against justice and a flame is carried by a man, a woman, a community, who lights a path of right action in the name of social change.

Burning passion. A slow burn. Coals. Smoke. On our hands and knees we blow the embers back to light. How close must we get to the source that burns to singe our souls into action?

A book of matches. Each turn of a page. *Strike moment.* A fire in the mind believing it is possible to read or paint the world differently.

The vision and match play of Chema Madoz is the endeavor of a true arsonist who is the artist who is the activist who understands the transformative power of fire.

The American West is burning, millions of acres are burning. It is the summer of 2000 with apocalyptic skies, where the sun glows red and round through gray-black clouds. The fire is now internal, moving underground.

What have we suppressed that has led us to this flame-jumping, blazing inferno?

Strike the match.

Stare into the flame.

Dare to be burned by the heat of our own ambitious hearts.

DESERT QUARTET

For Brooke
For the Duration

EARTH

Earth. Rock. Desert. I am walking barefoot on sand-stone, flesh responding to flesh. It is hot, so hot the rock threatens to burn through the calloused soles of my feet. I must quicken my pace, paying attention to where I step.

For as far as I can see, the canyon country of southern Utah extends in all directions. No compass can orient me here, only a pledge to love and walk the terrifying distances before me. What I fear and desire most in this world is passion. I fear it because it promises to be sponta-neous, out of my control, unnamed, beyond my reasonable self. I desire it because passion has color, like the landscape before me. It is not pale. It is not neutral. It reveals the backside of the heart.

I climb the slickrock on all fours, my hands and feet throbbing with the heat. It feels good to sweat, to be en-gaged, to inhabit my animal body.

My destination is Druid Arch (by way of the Joint Trail and Chesler Park), located in the southeastern corner of Canyonlands known as the Needles. I have no map, only cairns to guide me, the hand-stacked piles of rocks that say, "Trust me, turn here, I know the way."

Many resist cairns in the desert, kick them down, believing each traveler should walk on her own authority. It is also true, some cairns have been designed to fool people, to trick them off the trail so they will become lost forever, a quick lesson in self-reliance: to never believe in the stories of others. But I believe our desire to share is more potent and trustworthy than our desire to be alone. And so I do not anticipate these markers will lie. To walk in this country is always an act of faith.

The cairns I have followed have not secured my own path to intimacy as much as they have given me the courage to proceed—one foot in front of the other in a landscape mysterious, unpredictable, and vast. Nobody really knows the way, that is the myth of convention.

Cedar Mesa formations of sandstone envelop me. These pastel cliffs could convince you that you are a hostage with no way out. But the various shales, softer in character, create the slopes and benches that allow you to climb out of one canyon and into the heart of another.

Once I enter the Joint Trail, it is as though I am walking through the inside of an animal. It is dark, cool, and narrow with sheer sandstone walls on either side of me. I look up, a slit of sky above. Light is deceptive here. The palms of my hands search for a pulse in the rocks. I continue walking. In some places my hips can barely fit through. I turn sideways, my chest and back in a vise of geologic time.

I stop. The silence that lives in these sacred hallways presses against me. I relax. I surrender. I close my eyes. The arousal of my breath rises in me like music, like love, as the possessive muscles between my legs tighten and release. I come to the rock in a moment of stillness, giving and receiving, where there is no partition between my body and the body of Earth.

There are always logical explanations for the loss of one's mind in the desert. The parallel and intersecting maze I have been traveling through is tortured rock pulled apart by internal tensions and stresses that form fractures in Earth. These fractures become susceptible to erosion, creating deep slots between fins of sandstone.

Through the weathering of our spirit, the erosion of our soul, we are vulnerable. Isn't that what passion is—bodies broken open through change? We are acted upon. We invite and accept the life of another to take root inside. The succession of the canyons is like our own. A maidenhair fern hangs from the slickrock; water drips, drips, drips, until I catch it in my mouth. Drink deeply, the desert sighs.

For the next few miles I simply walk through the pastoral country of Chesler Park, meadows of serenity. This
landscape will take care of me. The open expanse of sky
makes me realize how necessary it is to live without words,
to be satisfied without answers, to simply be in a world
where there is no wind, no drama. To find a place of rest
and safety, no matter how fleeting it may be, no matter
how illusory, is to regain composure and locate bearings.
Picking up stones, I find myself adding to the cairns.

Elephant Canyon is composed of limestone ledges,
turquoise and lavender stairs that eventually lead desert
pilgrims to Druid Arch. The vegetation is lush; clumps of
milkweed, their orange inflorescence, attract monarchs in
migration. Willow, oak, and single-leaf ash provide cover
for collared lizards and towhees. Their shuffling in the dry
leaf litter reminds me of all I do not see. And the potholes,
sinks of water in the sandstone, beckon me down on hands
and knees for a closer look. The minutiae of mosquito and
mayfly larvae, fairy shrimp, tadpoles, and diving beetles is
swirling with its own sense of urgency. Perhaps this is the
mind of the lover, manic and driven, the shallow pools of
expectation that inevitably dry up.

Why, for most of us, is the vision of the erotic a rare
event, a shooting star, a flash flood, a moment of exotic
proportion and not in a stable condition?

In this tiny body of water in the desert, I detect waves. I
think of the ocean, wave after wave breaking on shore in

interminable monotony, yet witnessed, one by one, they can hold us in trance for hours.

The afternoon has delivered me to Druid Arch. Nothing has prepared me for this insistence of being, the pure artistry of shape and form standing quietly, magnificently in the canyons of Utah. Red rock. Blue sky. This arch is structured metamorphosis. Once a finlike tower, it has been perforated by a massive cave-in, responsible now for the keyholes where wind enters and turns. What has been opened, removed, eroded away is as compelling to me as what remains. Druid Arch—inorganic matter—rock rising from the desert floor as a creation of time, weathered, broken, and beautiful.

I touch the skin of my face. It seems so callow. Moving my fingers over the soft flesh that covers my cheekbones, I wonder what it means to be human and why, at this particular moment, rock seems more accessible and yielding than my own species.

WATER

At first I think it is a small leather pouch someone has dropped along the trail. I bend down, pick it up, and only then recognize it for what it is—a frog, dead and dried. I have a leather thong in my pack, which I take and thread through the frog's mouth and out through its throat. The skin is thin, which makes a quick puncture possible. I then slide the frog to the center of the thong, tie a knot with both ends, and create a necklace, which I wear.

I grew up with frogs. My brothers and cousins hurled them against canyon walls as we hiked the trail to Rainbow Bridge when Lake Powell was rising behind Glen Canyon Dam.

I hated what they did and told them so. But my cries only encouraged them, excited them, until I became the wall they would throw frogs against. I didn't know what to do—stand still and soften their blow by trying to catch each frog in my hands like a cradle, or turn and run, hoping they would miss me altogether. I tried to believe that somehow the frogs would sail through the air in safety, landing perfectly poised on a bed of moss. But, inevitably, the tiny canyon frogs, about the size of a ripe plum, quickly became entombed in the fists of adolescents and would die on impact, hitting my body, the boys' playing field. I would turn and walk down to the creek and wash the splattered remains off me. I would enter the water, sit down in the current, and release the frog bodies downstream with my tears.

I never forgave.

Years later, my impulse to bathe with frogs is still the same. Havasu. It is only an hour or so past dawn. The creek is cold and clear. I take off my skin of clothes and leave them on the bank. I shiver. How long has it been since I have allowed myself to lie on my back and float? The dried frog floats with me. A slight tug around my neck makes me believe it is still alive, swimming in the current. Travertine terraces spill over with turquoise water and we are held in place by a liquid hand that cools and calms the desert.

I dissolve. I am water. Only my face is exposed like an apparition over ripples. Playing with water. Do I dare? My legs open. The rushing water turns my body and touches me with a fast finger that does not tire. I receive without apology. Time. Nothing to rush, only to feel. I feel time in me. It is endless pleasure in the current. No control. No thought. Simply, here. My left hand reaches for the frog dangling from my neck, floating above my belly, and I hold it between my breasts like a withered heart, beating inside me, inside the river. We are moving downstream. Water. Water music. Blue notes, white notes, my body mixes with the body of water like jazz, the currents like jazz. I too am free to improvise.

I grip stones in shallow water. There is moss beneath my fingernails.

I leave the creek and walk up to my clothes. I am already dry. My skirt and blouse slip on effortlessly. I twist my hair and secure it with a stick. The frog is still with me. Do I imagine beads of turquoise have replaced the sunken and hollow eyes?

We walk. Canyons within canyons. The sun threatens to annihilate me. I recall all the oven doors I have opened to a blast of heat that burned my face. My eyes narrow. Each turn takes us deeper inside the Grand Canyon, my frog and I.

We are witnesses to this opening of time, vertical and horizontal at once. Between these crossbars of geology is a silent sermon on how the world was formed. Seas advanced and retreated. Dunes now stand in stone. Volcanoes erupted and lava cooled. Garnets shimmer and separate schist from granite. It is sculptured time to be touched, even tasted, our mineral content preserved in the desert.

This is the Rio Colorado.

We are water. We are swept away. Desire begins in wetness. My fingers curl around this little frog. Like me, it was born out of longing, wet, not dry. We can always return to our place of origin. Water. Water music. We are baptized by immersion, nothing less can replenish or restore our capacity to love. It is endless if we believe in water.

We are approaching a cliff. Red monkey flowers bloom. White-throated swifts and violet-green swallows crisscross above. My throat is parched. There is a large pool below. My fear of heights is overcome by my desire to merge. I dive into the water, deeper and deeper, my eyes open, and I see a slender passageway. I wonder if I have enough breath to venture down. Down. I take the risk and swim through the limestone corridor where the water is milky and I can barely focus through the shimmering sediments of sand until it opens into a clear, green room. The frog fetish floats to the surface. I rise too and grab a few breaths held in the top story of this strange cavern. I bump my head on the jagged ceiling. The green room turns red, red, my own blood, my own heart beating, my fingers touch the crown of my head and streak the wall.

Down. I sink back into the current, which carries me out of the underwater maze to the pool. I rise once again, feeling a scream inside me surfacing as I do scream, breathe, tread water, get my bearings. The outside world is green is blue is red is hot, so hot. I swim to a limestone ledge, climb out and lie on my stomach, breathing. The rock is steaming. The frog is under me. Beating. Heart beating. I am dry. I long to be wet. I am bleeding. Back on my knees, I immerse my head in the pool once more to ease the cut and look below. Half in. Half out. Amphibious. I am drawn to both earth and water. The frog breaks free from the leather thong. I try to grab its body but miss and watch it slowly spiral into the depths.

Before leaving, I drink from a nearby spring and hold a mouthful—I hear frogs, a chorus of frogs, their voices rising like bubbles from what seems to be the green room. Muddled at first, they become clear. I run back to the edge of the pool and listen. Throwing back my head, I burst into laughter spraying myself with water.

It is rain.

It is frogs.

It is hearts breaking against the bodies of those we love.

FIRE

I strike a match and light the shreds of kindling I have cut with my knife. Juniper. I fan the incense toward me. The smoke rises, curls, coils around my face. It feels good to be in the desert again. Home—where I can pause, remain silent. There is nothing to explain.

I break twigs and lean them against each other in the formation of a teepee. More smoke. On hands and knees in red sand, I blow at its base, blow again, add a handful of dried cottonwood leaves, blow, they ignite, flames engulf the triangle.

I sit back on my haunches, pleased that the fire is growing in the desert, in me, so that I can dream, remember, how it is that I have come to love. It is fate that determines the territory of the heart. I add more sticks, blow; the fire flares in darkness.

The wood opens.

Flames rise, flicker. My eyes blur. I hold every detail of love in my body, nothing forgotten, put more sticks on the fire. It surges, sputters, and purrs. The fire holds me captive, charismatic flames wave me closer. I add two more sticks like bodies to love. They are consumed instantly. The fire shifts, then settles with new intensity; it shifts again, adjusts. The wood pops like vertebrae. The silver bark of juniper burns black, turns white. A spark breathes.

I crouch down and blow on embers. They flare and quiver. I blow again. They become rubies. I reach into the coals, believing, and burn my fingers, blister their tips, pull back in pain and bury my hands in the sand. The fire wanes. I cannot bear its absence. I lower my head and blow. The fire ignites. My longing returns. When we want everything to change we call on fire.

I fetch more wood. Bones of piñon and juniper lie on the desert floor. Even in darkness I see them illumined by the moon. I gather them in my arms. This time they are larger. I must break them over my knee and feed the fire once again. The fire is aroused. The flames reach higher. I stand before them with my arms raised, my hands surrender and come down to caress the heat and mold it into faces I love. Do I dare to feel the white heat of my heart as a prayer? What is smoldering inside me? And how is it that pleasure exists between such beauty and violence? Feed the fire. No. Yes. My fingers touch the blaze of bodies in flames.

The fire explodes. Flames become blue tongues curling around each other. My eyes close. I step forward. My legs open to the heat, the tingling return of heat, inside, outside, shadows dance on the sandstone, my ghostly lover. I allow myself to be ravished. My generosity becomes my humiliation. The hair between my legs is singed. My left hand shields my face from the fire. Fingers open. It is a shuttered scape. Fingers clench. I hold a fist before the flames, loyal and disloyal at once.

Above me, free-tailed bats circle the flames like moths. Moths frighten me. I hate their addiction to light. But bats delight in darkness with their ears wide open. What do they hear that I am missing? Gifted in the location of echoes, they listen twice to all that is spoken in the desert. They are the dark angels who register our longings and pinpoint the cries lodged within our throats.

Heat. More heat. My face flushes red. The fire's hands are circling. I sit inches away from something that tomorrow will not exist. The blue-eyed coals I gaze into will disappear. Ashes. Ashes. Death is the natural conclusion of love.

But tonight it remains alive and I know in the shock of my heart that love is as transitory as fire. The warmth I feel, the glow of my body and the force of my own interior heat, is enough to keep me here.

It is our nature to be aroused—not once, but again and again. Where do we find the strength not to be pulled

apart by our passions? How do we inhabit the canyons inside a divided heart? One body. Two bodies. Three.

Beyond the junipers and piñons of this starless night, I
face the deep stare of darkness. This wildness cannot be
protected or preserved. There is little forgiveness here. Experience is the talisman I hold for courage. It is the desert
that persuades me toward love, to step outside and defy
custom one more time.

The fire now bears the last testament to trees. I blow
into the religious caverns of wood and watch them burn
brightly. My breath elucidates each yellow room and I remember the body as sacrament.

I have brought white candles with me. I take them out
of my pouch and secure them in the sand. With a small
stick I carry a flame from the fire and light one, and another, and another. They threaten to flicker and fade. I
shelter them with my hands and watch the way the wax
trickles down the side of each taper. Once away from the
flame, it hardens. My body reflects back the heat. I dip the
tip of my finger into the small basin of heated wax shining
at the base of the wick, bring it to my lips and paint them.

I turn toward the flames.

AIR

I hear it coming up through the rocks. It is a geyser of air that draws me farther up the red stone staircase. I look down over my shoulder to the river valley below and almost lose my nerve, but something pulls me higher, takes hold of my spine and stretches me.

I am not alone. Handprints are stamped on the staircase walls. I mime my hands against theirs. The Anasazi have never left.

I kneel at the mouth where the rock lips open, a column of wind is wafting, rushing up from the center of Earth. I try to shape a voice, to feel its words through the delicacy of my fingers, but it is not to be touched. My hands are pushed back by its force until my mouth is covered.

In the beginning, there were no words.

I am behind the rocks. I strain to see what it is, who it is, try to blow it out like a candle flame to see if a trail of smoke will curl and wrap itself around me, offering clues to how it moves in the world. But it is not to be seen.

There is nothing to taste.

There is nothing to smell.

I inch back, precarious, and focus on breath. Inhale. Exhale. Inhale. Exhale. The attention of breath in love, two breaths creating a third, mingling and shaping each other like clouds, cumulus clouds over the desert. On my back, I reclaim the sweet and simple ecstasy of breathing. The wind becomes a wail, a proper lament for all that is hidden. Inhale. Exhale. This is the dreamtime of the desert, the beginning of poetry.

My body softens as I make my wish to follow my breath. It settles on the backs of swallowtails. We are carried effortlessly through the labyrinth of these labial canyons.

Breath becomes a lizard, hands splayed on redrock walls. Up and down. Up and down. A raven lands, black wings are extended like arms.

The Animals know.

The Anasazi know.

It is audible.

I lean forward and listen. Breath. With my hands on the rocks, I place my mouth over the opening. My belly rises and falls. I move away and listen. I return with my mouth over the opening. Inhale. Exhale. I move away. I

listen. I return. I am dizzy. I am drunk with pleasure.
There is no need to speak.

    Listen.

    Below us.

    Above us.

    Inside us.

    Come.

    This is all there is.

WILD MERCY

The eyes of the future are looking back at us and they are praying for us to see beyond our own time. They are kneeling with hands clasped that we might act with restraint, that we might leave room for the life that is destined to come. To protect what is wild is to protect what is gentle. Perhaps the wildness we fear is the pause between our own heartbeats, the silent space that says we live only by grace. Wilderness lives by this same grace. Wild mercy is in our hands.

Appendices

America's Redrock Wilderness Act

Map of America's Redrock Wilderness

America's Redrock Wilderness: The Citizens' Proposal

Supporting Organizations

AMERICA'S REDROCK WILDERNESS ACT

(Abridged)

107th Congress
1st Session

HR 1613

*To designate certain Federal land in the State of Utah as
wilderness, and for other purposes.*

In the House of Representatives

April 26, 2001

Mr. HINCHEY (for himself, Mr. MORAN of Virginia, Mr.
BROWN of Ohio, Mr. BOUCHER, Mr. TIERNEY, Mr.
BONIOR, Mr. PRICE of North Carolina, Ms. BALDWIN, Mr.
PALLONE, Mr. CAPUANO, Mrs. MALONEY of New York,
Mr. FILNER, Mr. MARKEY, Mr. PASCRELL, Mr. LEVIN,
Mrs. MCCARTHY of New York, Mr. MCDERMOTT, Ms.
BROWN of Florida, Mr. DELAHUNT, Mr. SHAYS, Ms.
HOOLEY of Oregon, Ms. KILPATRICK, Mrs. TAUSCHER,
Mr. SANDERS, Mr. MALONEY of Connecticut, Mr. BLA-
GOJEVICH, Mr. SERRANO, Mr. ALLEN, Mr. STARK, Mr.

BORSKI, Mr. BRADY of Pennsylvania, Mrs. CAPPS, Ms.
WOOLSEY, Mr. BAIRD, Mr. DEFAZIO, Mr. MCNULTY,
Ms. DELAURO, Mr. JACKSON of Illinois, Mr. MCGOV-
ERN, Mr. BECERRA, Ms. LEE, Mr. WEINER, Mr. SHER-
MAN, Mr. WYNN, Mr. PAYNE, Mr. SMITH of Washington,
Mr. COYNE, Mr. UDALL of Colorado, Mr. CLAY, Mr. CON-
YERS, Mr. HOLT, Mr. EVANS, Mr. KUCINICH, Mr. NEAL
of Massachusetts, Mrs. MEEK of Florida, Mr. GONZALEZ,
Mr. FATTAH, Mr. BENTSEN, Mr. MATSUI, Mr. SMITH of
New Jersey, Mr. REYES, Mr. INSLEE, Mr. OLVER, Mr.
HILLIARD, Mr. SAWYER, Mr. MOORE, Mr. LEWIS of
Georgia, Mrs. JONES of Ohio, Mr. HALL of Ohio, Mr.
LUTHER, Mr. THOMPSON of Mississippi, Mr. GEORGE
MILLER of California, Mr. KLECZKA, Mrs. NAPOLI-
TANO, Mr. DEUTSCH, Mr. KILDEE, Mr. HOEFFEL, Mr.
FERGUSON, Ms. ROYBAL-ALLARD, Ms. RIVERS, Mr.
WAXMAN, Mr. CROWLEY, Mr. MEEHAN, Mr. WEXLER,
Mr. SIMMONS, Ms. WATERS, Mr. CARDIN, Mr. NADLER,
Mrs. MINK of Hawaii, Ms. MCCOLLUM, Ms. DEGETTE,
Mr. BLUMENAUER, Ms. SCHAKOWSKY, Mr. AN-
DREWS, Ms. MCCARTHY of Missouri, Ms. KAPTUR,
Ms. ESHOO, Mr. ENGEL, Ms. VELAZQUEZ, Mrs. LOWEY,
Ms. BERKLEY, Mr. LANGEVIN, Mr. MENENDEZ, Mr.
TOWNS, Mrs. KELLY, Ms. EDDIE BERNICE JOHNSON
of Texas, Mr. SABO, Mr. DAVIS of Illinois, Mr. ROTHMAN,
Mr. KENNEDY of Rhode Island, Mr. FARR of California, Mr.
LEACH, Mr. THOMPSON of California, Mr. SPRATT, Mrs.

MORELLA, Mr. MURTHA, Mr. OWENS, Ms. MCKINNEY,
Ms. JACKSON-LEE of Texas, Mr. FRANK, Mr. CLEMENT,
Mr. ACKERMAN, Ms. MILLENDER-MCDONALD, Mr.
JEFFERSON, Mr. CLYBURN, Mr. HILL, Mr. BERMAN, Mr.
GUTIERREZ, Mr. UDALL of New Mexico, Mr. STRICK-
LAND, Mr. RUSH, Mr. HONDA, Mr. BARRETT, Mr. BAL-
DACCI, Mr. WU, Mr. CUMMINGS, Mr. FORD, Mr. MEEKS
of New York, Mr. LARSEN of Washington, Mrs. DAVIS of
California, Mr. PHELPS, Ms. SANCHEZ, Ms. LOFGREN,
Ms. CARSON of Indiana, and Ms. SOLIS) introduced the fol-
lowing bill; which was referred to the Committee on Resources

America's Red Rock Wilderness Act of 2001

A Bill
*To designate certain Federal land in the State of Utah as
wilderness, and for other purposes.*

Title I—Designation of Wilderness Areas
Sec. 101. Great Basin Wilderness Areas.

FINDINGS—Congress finds that—

(1) the Great Basin region of western Utah is comprised of
starkly beautiful mountain ranges that rise as islands from
the desert floor;

(2) the Wah Wah Mountains in the Great Basin region are arid and austere, with massive cliff faces and leathery slopes speckled with piñon and juniper;

(3) the Pilot Range and Stansbury Mountains in the Great Basin region are high enough to draw moisture from passing clouds and support ecosystems found nowhere else on earth;

(4) from bristlecone pine, the world's oldest living organism, to newly-flowered mountain meadows, mountains of the Great Basin region are islands of nature that support remarkable biological diversity; and provide opportunities to experience the colossal silence of the Great Basin; and

(5) the Great Basin region of western Utah should be protected and managed to ensure the preservation of the natural conditions of the region.

Sec. 102. Zion and Mojave Desert Wilderness Areas.

FINDINGS—Congress finds that—

(1) the renowned landscape of Zion National Park, including soaring cliff walls, forested plateaus, and deep narrow gorges, extends beyond the boundaries of the Park onto surrounding public lands managed by the Secretary;

(2) from the pink sand dunes of Moquith Mountain to the golden pools of Beaver Dam Wash, the Zion and Mojave Desert areas encompass three major provinces of the Southwest that include the sculpted canyon country of the Colorado Plateau; the Mojave Desert; and portions of the Great Basin;

(3) the Zion and Mojave Desert areas display a rich mosaic of biological, archaeological, and scenic diversity;

(4) one of the last remaining populations of threatened desert tortoise is found within this region; and

(5) the Zion and Mojave Desert areas in Utah should be protected and managed as wilderness areas.

Sec. 103. Grand Staircase–Escalante Wilderness Areas.

GRAND STAIRCASE AREA FINDINGS—Congress finds that—

(1) the area known as the Grand Staircase rises more than 6,000 feet in a series of great cliffs and plateaus from the depths of the Grand Canyon to the forested rim of Bryce Canyon;

(2) the Grand Staircase spans six major life zones, from the lower Sonoran Desert to the alpine forest; and encom-

passes geologic formations that display 3,000,000,000 years of Earth's history;

(3) land managed by the Secretary lines the intricate canyon system of the Paria River and forms a vital natural corridor connection to the deserts and forests of these national parks;

(4) land described above (other than Upper Kanab Creek, Moquith Mountain, and Vermillion Cliffs) is located within the Grand Staircase–Escalante National Monument; and

(5) the Grand Staircase in Utah should be protected and managed as a wilderness area.

KAIPAROWITS PLATEAU FINDINGS—Congress finds that—

(1) the Kaiparowits Plateau east of the Paria River is one of the most rugged and isolated wilderness regions in the United States;

(2) the Kaiparowits Plateau, a windswept land of harsh beauty, contains distant vistas and a remarkable variety of plant and animal species;

(3) ancient forests, an abundance of big game animals, and 22 species of raptors thrive undisturbed on the grassland mesa tops of the Kaiparowits Plateau;

(4) each of the areas described above is located within the Grand Staircase–Escalante National Monument; and

(5) the Kaiparowits Plateau should be protected and managed as a wilderness area.

ESCALANTE CANYONS FINDINGS—Congress finds that—

(1) glens and coves carved in massive sandstone cliffs, spring-watered hanging gardens, and the silence of ancient Anasazi ruins are examples of the unique features that entice hikers, campers, and sightseers from around the world to Escalante Canyon;

(2) Escalante Canyon links the spruce fir forests of the 11,000-foot Aquarius Plateau with winding slickrock canyons that flow into Lake Powell;

(3) Escalante Canyon, one of Utah's most popular natural areas, contains critical habitat for deer, elk, and wild bighorn sheep that also enhances the scenic integrity of the area;

(4) each of the areas described in above is located within the Grand Staircase–Escalante National Monument; and

(5) Escalante Canyon should be protected and managed as a wilderness area.

Sec. 104. Moab-LaSal Canyons Wilderness Areas.

FINDINGS—Congress finds that—

(1) the canyons surrounding the LaSal Mountains and the town of Moab offer a variety of extraordinary landscapes;

(2) outstanding examples of natural formations and landscapes in the Moab-LaSal area include the huge sandstone fins of Behind the Rocks, the mysterious Fisher Towers, and the whitewater rapids of Westwater Canyon; and

(3) the Moab-LaSal area should be protected and managed as a wilderness area.

Sec. 105. Henry Mountains Wilderness Areas.

FINDINGS—Congress finds that—

(1) the Henry Mountain Range, the last mountain range to be discovered and named by early explorers in the contiguous United States, still retains a wild and undiscovered quality;

(2) fluted badlands that surround the flanks of 11,000-foot Mounts Ellen and Pennell contain areas of critical habitat for mule deer and for the largest herd of free-roaming buffalo in the United States;

(3) despite their relative accessibility, the Henry Mountain Range remains one of the wildest, least-known ranges in the United States; and

(4) the Henry Mountain range should be protected and managed to ensure the preservation of the range as a wilderness area.

Sec. 106. Glen Canyon Wilderness Areas.

FINDINGS—Congress finds that—

(1) the side canyons of Glen Canyon, including the Dirty Devil River and the Red, White and Blue Canyons, contain some of the most remote and outstanding landscapes in southern Utah;

(2) the Dirty Devil River, once the fortress hideout of outlaw Butch Cassidy's Wild Bunch, has sculpted a maze of slickrock canyons through an imposing landscape of monoliths and inaccessible mesas;

(3) the Red and Blue Canyons contain colorful Chinle/Moenkopi badlands found nowhere else in the region; and

(4) the canyons of Glen Canyon in the State should be protected and managed as wilderness areas.

Sec. 107. San Juan–Anasazi Wilderness Areas.

FINDINGS—Congress finds that—

(1) more than 1,000 years ago, the Anasazi Indian culture flourished in the slickrock canyons and on the piñon-covered mesas of southeastern Utah;

(2) evidence of the ancient presence of the Anasazi pervades the Cedar Mesa area of the San Juan–Anasazi area where cliff dwellings, rock art, and ceremonial kivas embellish sandstone overhangs and isolated benchlands;

(3) the Cedar Mesa area is in need of protection from the vandalism and theft of its unique cultural resources;

(4) the Cedar Mesa wilderness areas should be created to protect both the archaeological heritage and the extraordinary wilderness, scenic, and ecological values of the United States; and

(5) the San Juan–Anasazi area should be protected and managed as a wilderness area to ensure the preservation of the unique and valuable resources of that area.

Sec. 108. Canyonlands Basin Wilderness Areas.

FINDINGS—Congress finds that—

(1) Canyonlands National Park safeguards only a small portion of the extraordinary red-hued, cliff-walled canyon-land region of the Colorado Plateau;

(2) areas near Arches National Park and Canyonlands National Park contain canyons with rushing perennial streams, natural arches, bridges, and towers;

(3) the gorges of the Green and Colorado Rivers, lie on adjacent land managed by the Secretary;

(4) popular overlooks in Canyonlands National Park and Dead Horse Point State Park have views directly into adjacent areas, including Lockhart Basin and Indian Creek; and

(5) designation of these areas as wilderness would ensure the protection of this erosional masterpiece of nature and of the rich pockets of wildlife found within its expanded boundaries.

Sec. 109. San Rafael Swell Wilderness Areas.

FINDINGS—Congress finds that—

(1) the San Rafael Swell towers above the desert like a castle, ringed by 1,000-foot ramparts of Navajo Sandstone;

(2) the highlands of the San Rafael Swell have been fractured by uplift and rendered hollow by erosion over countless millennia, leaving a tremendous basin punctuated by mesas, buttes, and canyons and traversed by sediment-laden desert streams;

(3) among other places, the San Rafael wilderness offers exceptional back country opportunities in the colorful Wild Horse Badlands, the monoliths of North Caineville Mesa, the rock towers of Cliff Wash, and colorful cliffs of Humbug Canyon;

(4) the mountains within these areas are among Utah's most valuable habitat for desert bighorn sheep; and

(5) the San Rafael Swell area should be protected and managed to ensure its preservation as a wilderness area.

Sec. 110. Book Cliffs and Uinta Basin Wilderness Areas.

FINDINGS—Congress finds that—

(1) the Book Cliffs and Uinta Basin wilderness areas offer unique big game hunting opportunities in verdant high-plateau forests; the opportunity for float trips of several days duration down the Green River in Desolation Canyon; and the opportunity for calm water canoe weekends on the White River;

(2) the long rampart of the Book Cliffs bounds the area on the south, while seldom-visited uplands, dissected by the rivers and streams, slope away to the north into the Uinta Basin;

(3) bighorn sheep, elk, mule deer, bears, and cougars flourish in the back country of the Book Cliffs; and

(4) the Book Cliffs and Uinta Basin areas should be protected and managed to ensure the protection of the areas as wilderness.

THE CITIZENS' PROPOSAL FOR
AMERICA'S REDROCK WILDERNESS

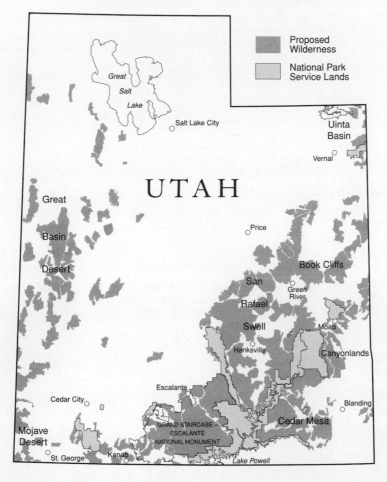

Proposed
Wilderness

National Park
Service Lands

Great
Salt
Lake

Salt Lake City

Uinta
Basin

Vernal

UTAH

Price

Great

Book Cliffs

Basin

San

Green
River

Desert

Rafael

Swell

Moab

Hanksville

Canyonlands

Escalante

Cedar City

Blanding

Mojave
Desert

GRAND STAIRCASE –
ESCALANTE
NATIONAL MONUMENT

Cedar Mesa

St. George

Kanab

Lake Powell

AMERICA'S REDROCK WILDERNESS: THE CITIZENS' PROPOSAL

Book Cliffs
Chipeta Cluster (95,000)
Desbrough Canyon (13,000)
Desolation Canyon (548,000)
Diamond Canyon (166,000)
Hideout Canyon (12,000)
Lower Bitter Creek (14,000)
Mexico Point (15,000)
Sunday School Canyon (18,000)
Survey Point (8000)
Turtle Canyon (37,000)
White River (25,000)
Winter Ridge (38,000)

Book Cliffs Region: 989,000 acres

Canyonlands Basin
Bridger Jack Mesa (33,000)
Butler Wash (27,000)
Dead Horse Cliffs (4100)

Demon's Playground (3700)

Duma Point (14,000)

Gooseneck (9000)

Hatch Point Canyons (149,000)

Horsethief Point (15,000)

Indian Creek (28,000)

Labyrinth Canyon (150,000)

San Rafael River (101,000)

Shay Mountain (14,000)

Sweetwater Reef (69,000)

Upper Horseshoe Canyon (60,000)

Canyonlands Basin Region: 676,800 acres

Dinosaur

Bourdette Draw (15,000)

Bull Canyon (2800)

Diamond Breaks (8000)

Diamond Mountain (27,000)

Goslin Mountain (4900)

Lower Flaming Gorge (20,000)

Moonshine Draw (10,000)

O-Wi-Yu-Kuts (13,000)

Red Creek Badlands (3600)

Dinosaur Region: 104,300 acres

Glen Canyon

Cane Spring Desert (18,000)
Dark Canyon (134,000)
Dirty Devil (242,000)
Fiddler Butte (92,000)
Flat Tops (30,000)
Little Rockies (64,000)
Red Rock Plateau (213,000)
White Canyon (98,000)

Glen Canyon Region: 891,000 acres

Grand Staircase

Andalex Not (18,000)
The Blue (21,000)
Box Canyon (2800)
Brinkerhof Flats (3000)
Bryce View (4500)
Bunting Point (10,000)
Burning Hills (80,000)
Carcass Canyon (83,000)
Colt Mesa (28,000)
Death Hollow (49,000)
East of Bryce (750)
Fiftymile Bench (12,000)
Fiftymile Mountain (203,000)

Forty Mile Gulch (6600)

Heaps Canyon (4000)

Horse Spring Canyon (31,000)

Hurricane Wash (9000)

Kodachrome Headlands (10,000)

Ladder Canyon (14,000)

Lampstand (8000)

Little Valley Canyon (4100)

Moquith Mountain (16,000)

Mud Spring Canyon (65,000)

Muley Twist Flank (3600)

Nephi Point (14,000)

Nipple Bench (32,000)

North Escalante Canyons (176,000)

Paria Wilderness Expansion (3300)

Paria–Hackberry (188,000)

Pine Hollow (11,000)

Pioneer Mesa (11,000)

Rock Cove (16,000)

Scorpion (53,000)

Slopes of Bryce (2600)

Sooner Bench (390)

Steep Creek (35,000)

Studhorse Peaks (24,000)

Timber Mountain (51,000)

Upper Kanab Creek (49,000)

Vermillion Cliffs (26,000)
Paradise Canyon–Wahwea (262,000)
Warm Creek (23,000)
Wide Hollow (6800)
Willis Creek (21,000)

Grand Staircase Region: 1,666,740 acres

Great Basin
Barn Hills (20,000)
Black Hills (9000)
Bullgrass Knoll (15,000)
Burbank Hills/Tunnel Springs (92,000)
Cedar Mountains (108,000)
Conger Mountain (21,000)
Crater Bench (35,000)
Crater and Silver Island (121,000)
Cricket Mountains Cluster (62,000)
Deep Creek Mountains (125,000)
Drum Mountains (39,000)
Dugway Mountains (24,000)
Fish Springs Mountains (64,000)
Granite Peak (19,000)
Grassy Mountains (23,000)
Grouse Creek Mountains (15,000)
House Range (190,000)

Keg Mountains (38,000)
King Top (110,000)
Ledger Canyon (9000)
Little Goose Creek (1200)
Middle/Granite Mountains (80,000)
Mountain Home Range (88,000)
Newfoundland Mountains (22,000)
Oquirrih Mountains (8000)
Ochre Mountain (13,000)
Painted Rock Mountain (26,000)
Paradise/Steamboat Mountain (145,000)
Pilot Range (45,000)
Red Tops (28,000)
Rockwell–Little Sahara (12,000)
San Francisco Mountains (39,000)
Sand Ridge (73,000)
Simpson Mountains (42,000)
Snake Valley (100,000)
Stansbury Mountains (24,000)
Thomas Range (36,000)
Tule Valley (159,000)
Wah Wah Mountains (167,000)
Wasatch/Sevier Plateaus (29,000)
White Rock Range (5200)

Great Basin Region: 2,281,400 acres

Henry Mountains
Bull Mountain (16,000)
Bullfrog Creek (35,000)
Dogwater Creek (3200)
Fremont Gorge (20,000)
Long Canyon (16,000)
Mount Ellen–Blue Hills (140,000)
Mount Hillers (21,000)
Mount Pennell (147,000)
Notom Bench (6200)
Ragged Mountain (28,000)

Henry Mountains Region: 432,400 acres

Hot Desert–Zion
Beaver Dam Mountains (30,000)
Beaver Dam Wash (23,000)
Beaver Dam Wilderness (8000)
Canaan Mountain (67,000)
Cottonwood Canyon (12,000)
Cougar Canyon/Doc's Pass (41,000)
Joshua Tree (12,000)
Mount Escalante (17,000)
Parunuweap Canyon (43,000)
Red Butte (4500)
Red Mountain (21,000)

Scarecrow Peak (16,000)
Zion Adjacent (56,000)

Hot Desert–Zion Region: 350,500 acres

Moab–LaSals
Beaver Creek (38,000)
Behind the Rocks and Hunter's Canyon (22,000)
Big Triangle (20,000)
Dome Plateau–Professor Valley (35,000)
Fisher Towers (18,000)
Goldbar Canyon (6500)
Granite Creek (4900)
Mary Jane Canyon (25,000)
Mill Creek Canyon (14,000)
Porcupine Rim and Morning Glory Canyon (20,000)
Westwater Canyon (37,000)
Yellow Bird (4200)

Moab–LaSal Region: 244,600 acres

San Juan–Anasazi
Allen Canyon (5900)
Arch Canyon (30,000)
Comb Ridge (15,000)
East Montezuma (45,000)

Fish and Owl Creek Canyons (73,000)
Grand Gulch (159,000)
Hammond Canyon (4400)
Nokai Dome (93,000)
Road Canyon (63,000)
San Juan River (15,000)
The Tabernacle (7000)

San Juan–Anasazi Region: 510,300 acres

San Rafael Swell
Cedar Mountain (15,000)
Devil's Canyon (23,000)
Hondu Canyon (20,000)
Jones Bench (2800)
Limestone Cliffs (25,000)
Lost Spring Wash (37,000)
Mexican Mountain (100,000)
Molen Reef (33,000)
Muddy Creek (240,000)
Mussentuchit Badlands (25,000)
Price River–Humbug (98,000)
Red Desert (40,000)
Rock Canyon (18,000)
San Rafael Reef (114,000)
Sid's Mountain (107,000)

Upper Muddy Creek (19,000)
Wild Horse Mesa (92,000)

San Rafael Swell Region: 1,067,800 acres

America's Redrock Wilderness: 9,286,640 acres

SUPPORTING ORGANIZATIONS

Bluff City Historic Preservation Association
P.O. Box 76
Bluff, UT 84512

California Wilderness Coalition
2655 Portage Bay East, Suite 5
Davis, CA 95616
Phone: 530-758-0380
www.calwild.org

Canyonlands Natural History Association
3031 S Highway 191
Moab, UT 84532
Phone: 435-259-6003
www.cnha.org

Castle Rock Collaboration
HC 64, Box 2903
Castle Valley, UT 84532
www.castlerockcollaboration.org

Glen Canyon Action Network
P.O. Box 466
21 North Main
Moab, UT 84532
Phone: 435-259-1063
www.info@drainit.org

Glen Canyon Institute (Flagstaff Office)
P.O. Box 1925
Flagstaff, AZ 86002-1925
Phone: 520-556-9311
www.glencanyon.org

Grand Canyon Trust
2601 N. Fort Valley Road
Flagstaff, AZ 86001
Phone: 520-774-7488
www.grandcanyontrust.org

Great Old Broads for Wilderness
P.O. Box 2206
Cedar City, UT 845721
Phone: 435-867-0704
www.greatoldbroads.org

Pew Wilderness Center
Wayburn Wilderness House
122 C Street, N.W.
Washington, D.C. 20001
Phone: 202-544-3691
www.pewwildernesscenter.org

Sierra Club (San Francisco Office)
85 Second Street, 2nd floor
San Francisco, CA 94105
Phone: 415-977-5500
www.sierraclub.org

Sierra Club (Utah Chapter)
2273 S Highland Drive
Salt Lake City, UT 84106
Phone: 801-467-9294
www.wildutah.org

Southern Utah Wilderness Alliance (Moab Office)
P.O. Box 968
Moab, UT 84532
Phone: 435-259-5440
www.suwa.org

Southern Utah Wilderness Alliance (Salt Lake City Office)
1471 South 1100 East
Salt Lake City, UT 84105
Phone: 801-486-7639, ext. 20
www.suwa.org

Southern Utah Wilderness Alliance (Washington, D.C., Office)
122 C Street N.W., Suite 240
Washington, D.C. 20001
Phone: 202-546-2215
www.suwa.org

The Nature Conservancy (Moab Office)
P.O. Box 1329
Moab, UT 84532
Phone: 435-259-4629
www.nature.org

The Nature Conservancy (Utah Office)
559 E. South Temple
Salt Lake City, UT 84102
Phone: 801-531-0999
www.nature.org

Utah Open Lands
1790 South 1100 East, Suite 3
Salt Lake City, UT 84105
Phone: 801-463-6156
www.utahopenlands.org

Redrock Forests
90 W Center St.
Moab, UT 84532
Phone: 435-259-1667
www.redrockforests.org

Wasatch Mountain Club
1390 S 1100 E, #103
Salt Lake City, UT 84105
Phone: 801-463-9842
www.wasatchmountainclub.org

The Wilderness Society (Denver Office)
7475 Dakin Street, Suite 410
Denver, CO 80221
Phone: 303-650-5818

The Wilderness Society (Washington, D.C., Office)
1615 M Street, NW
Washington, DC 20036
Phone: 202-833-2300
www.wilderness.org

Utah Wilderness Coalition
P.O. Box 520974
Salt Lake City, UT 84152
Phone: 801-486-2872
www.xmission.com\~wildutah\

Zion Natural History Association
Zion National Park
Springdale, UT 84767
Phone: 435-772-3265
www.zionpark.org

ACKNOWLEDGMENTS

I wish to acknowledge the following people who have been in some way collaborators on *Red:*

The vision of photographer John Telford, for his original work on *Coyote's Canyon;* Mary Frank for the beauty and physicality of her art in *Desert Quartet;* Stephen Trimble and Trent Alvey, creative partners who helped make *Testimony: Writers Speak on Behalf of Utah Wilderness,* a chapbook presented to the United States Congress in September 1995, and Emily Buchwald, who published it one year later through Milkweed Press. And, of course, I want to heartfully thank the community of writers in the American West who contributed their smart and soulful writings so graciously to that anthology.

A special acknowledgment goes to the following editors with whom I had the pleasure of working, whose skills sharpened my words and ideas: Deb Clow at *Northern Lights Magazine;* Casey Walker of the *Wild Duck Review;* Jean Wyss at *Outside for Women;* Deborah Kirk at *Harper's Bazaar;* Lily Pond at *Yellow Silk;* Roger Cohn at *Audubon;* Nora Garrigue with the *Patagonia* catalog; Tom Butler at *Wild Earth;* Brendan Lemon at *The New Yorker;*

Steven Madoff at *Time Magazine*, Barbara Payne at National Geographic Books; Michael Millman at Viking Penguin Books; Barbara Ras at the University of Georgia Press; and Curt Meine at the University of Wisconsin Press; and Andy Nettell at Music of Moab.

Adrienne and Sam Taylor were gracious enough to let me reprint "Police Report" from their weekly paper, *The Moab Times Independent*.

One of my great joys has been the opportunity to work closely with conservation groups in Utah. Without their help and vigilance, Utah wildlands would be much more vulnerable. I thank Mike Matz, Scott Groene, Cindy Shogan, Tom Price, Ken Rait, Amy Irving, Herb McHarg, Liz Thomas, Heidi McIntosh, Dave Pacheco, Keith Hammond, Kevin Walker, Diane Kelly, Amy Barry, Erin Moore, Liz McCoy, Christy Calvin, Lindsay Oswald, Ray Bloxham, Gail Hoskisson, Susan Tixier, Brandt Calken, Larry Young, and the entire staff and board of directors of the Southern Utah Wilderness Alliance; Dave Livermore, Chris Montague, Libby Ellis, Joel Peterson, Sue Bellagamba, Anne Wilson, and Joel Tuhy of the Utah chapter of The Nature Conservancy; Julie Mack of the North Fork Preservation Alliance; Eleanor Bliss, Bill Hedden, and Jeff Barnard of the Grand Canyon Trust; Jim Caitlin, and dear friends and neighbors of the Castle Rock Collaboration, especially Laura Kamala and Dave Erley.

I want to thank Fred Swanson who is responsible for

the fine map of America's Redrock Wilderness. He is also the editor and author of *America's Redrock Wilderness— Protecting a National Treasure,* an important resource for those interested in learning more about this area.

Chalk Butte Digital Maps in Boulder, Wyoming, created the endsheets from their map of the Colorado Plateau.

Mike Nelson from Anasazi State Park, Deborah A. Westfall, museum curator at Edge of the Cedars State Park, and archaeologist Erik Ferland, were all extraordinarily helpful in securing material regarding the scarlet macaw feather sash. I am grateful for their expertise and enthusiasm. And to Kent Frost, the discoverer of the sash.

And Ayako Harvie, Kristen Bearse, Diane Kelly, José Knighton, and Ann Floor advised and oversaw many of the details required to complete this book. My gratitude to Fearn Cutler de Vicq de Cumptich for the integrity of her book design and to Archie Ferguson for the design of the jacket.

Dan Frank, my editor at Pantheon Books took this book on faith, having never been to the redrock country of southern Utah, and then at its completion chose to bring his family to visit. Magic.

Carl Brandt, my agent and friend, is Coyoté extraordinaire.

And, of course, my love to Brooke Williams, water in the desert.

The great silences of the desert are not void of sound,
but void of distractions.

One day, this landscape will take
the language out of me.

TTW

The section "Desert Quartet" was originally published in slightly different form as the book *Desert Quartet* by Pantheon Books, a division of Random House, Inc., New York, 1995. The section "Coyote's Canyon" was originally published in slightly different form by Peregrine Smith, Layton, 1989. Some of the stories in the section "Red" originally appeared in the following publications: "Bloodlines" in *Testimony: Writers Speak on Behalf of Utah Wilderness,* Milkwood Editions. • "To Be Taken" in *The Iowa Review*. • "The Erotic Landscape" in *Yellow Silk*. • "A Letter to Deb Clow" in *Northern Lights*. • "Red" in *The Wild Duck Review*. • "Ode to Slowness" in *Outside for Women*. • "Labor" first appeared as "The Birthing Rock" in *Heart of a Nation,* National Geographic Society. • "Mary Austin's Ghost" first appeared as the Introduction in *The Land of Little Rain,* Penguin Books. • "Wilderness and Intellectual Humility: Aldo Leopold" in *The Essential Aldo Leopold,* University of Wisconsin Press. • "A Prayer for a Wild Millennium" in *Patagonia*.

A NOTE ABOUT THE AUTHOR

Terry Tempest Williams is the author of *Refuge: An Unnatural History of Family and Place,* now considered a classic in environmental literature. Her other books include *Pieces of White Shell; Coyote's Canyon; An Unspoken Hunger; Desert Quartet;* and most recently, *Leap.* Her work has appeared in *The New Yorker, The Nation, Outside, Audubon, Parabola,* the *Utne Reader, The Iowa Review,* and *Best American Essays.* She has been a fellow of the John Simon Guggenheim Memorial Foundation and the Lannan Foundation in creative nonfiction, and a recipient of the Lila Wallace-Reader's Digest Award. She lives with her husband, Brooke Williams, in Grand County, Utah.

A NOTE ON THE TYPE

This book was set in Granjon, which is named in honor of the great sixteenth-century printer, publisher, and type founder Roberto Granjon. The type, however, is based on models by Claude Garamond, Granjon's teacher, who established the first type foundry, and whose fonts remain among the most beautiful and legible ever cut.

Composed by MD Linocomp
Westminster, MD

Printed and bound by
R. R. Donnelley & Sons Company,
Bloomsburg, PA

A NOTE ABOUT THE IMAGE
APPEARING ON THE JACKET SPINE

Item: Ancestral Puebloan sash
Provenance: Lavender Canyon, southeast Utah
Date: Circa A.D. 920
Dimensions: 49.5 cm. × 29 cm.
Description: Yucca fiber cords, wrapped with more than
2,000 scarlet macaw feathers, attached to a
pelt made from an indigenous American
Southwest tassel-eared squirrel

The scarlet macaw, whose plumage is colored red, scarlet, crimson, chrome yellow, and blue, is indigenous to the humid lowlands of southern Mexico. Its feathers were transported to the arid American Southwest via a wide-ranging prehistoric trade network that thrived from approximately A.D. 1050 to A.D. 1200. Red is the Puebloan color for south, the home of the sun; hence, the scarlet macaw is symbolically affiliated with the Puebloan ritual landscape. Often used to embellish religious objects, the scarlet macaw feathers in this sash indicate that it is a ceremonial garment. Similar sashes, made of red cloth, are worn today by Hopi and Zuni dancers during seasonal *kachina* ceremonies, emphasizing the continuity of ancient and modern Pueblo cultures.

Unique in its provenance, integrity, materials, and style, this ancient sash exemplifies the interrelatedness of nature, color, symbolism, and belief expressed in ancestral Puebloan craftsmanship, art, and culture.